THE EVOLUTION OF CRIMINOLOGY

THE EVOLUTION OF CRIMINOLOGY

William V. Pelfrey, Ph.D.

Department of Criminal Justice
University of Alabama in Birmingham

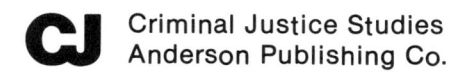

CJ Criminal Justice Studies
Anderson Publishing Co.

THE EVOLUTION OF CRIMINOLOGY
Copyright © 1980 by Anderson Publishing Company
All rights reserved. No part of this book may be used or reproduced by any means without written permission from the publisher.
Library of Congress Catalog Number: 79-55204
ISBN: 0-87084-698-1
The project editor for this book was Candice Piaget, Anderson Publishing Co.
Cover designed by Steve Faske

The material in this project was prepared under Grant number 78-NI-AX-0050 from Law Enforcement Assistance Administration, U.S. Department of Justice. Researchers undertaking such projects under government sponsorship are encouraged to express freely their professional judgment. Therefore, points of view or opinions stated in this document do not necessarily represent the official position or policy of the U.S. Department of Justice.

Contents

1. THE PROGRESSION OF CRIMINOLOGICAL THOUGHT
   The Classical School of Criminology   2-5
   The Positive School of Criminology   5-11
   The Evolution of Criminological Theories   11-13
   Sociology of Criminology   13-14
   The Dominant Paradigm: Functional or Conflict?   15-20
     Functionalism   15-17
     Conflict Perspective   17-20

2. EARLY CRIMINOLOGICAL THEORIES
   Biological Theories   21-27
   Psychological Theories   27-31
   Sociological Theories   31-49
     Control Theory   32-36
     Strain Theory   36-41
     Cultural Deviance Theory   41-43
     Symbolic Interactionist Theories   43-49

3. THE NEW CRIMINOLOGY: A REVIEW OF THE LITERATURE
   Criminal Justice   51-53
   Perspectives Within the New Criminology   53-91
     Conflict Theory as a Basis of the New Criminology   54-60
     Conflict Criminology   60-73
     Critical Criminology   73-87
     Radical Criminology   87-91
   Criticisms of the New Criminology   91-95
   Conclusion: The Future of Criminology   95-98

   REFERENCES   99-109

   INDEX   111-117

1. The Progression of Criminological Thought

Thomas Hobbes, the seventeenth century social philosopher, proclaimed that human society, in its natural state, was one of "continual fear and danger of violent death; and the life of man, solitary, poor, nasty, brutish, and short." In light of this statement sociologists ask how can there be any semblance of social order, and more generally, how is society itself possible. They confront questions such as: Why do people fall into patterns of crimes? What does an individual's family life have to do with his decision to be either a lawful member of society or a criminal? What rationales lie behind a society's methods of control and punishment of deviants? In short, sociologists grapple with the artificial confines necessary for social order and the effects those confines have on individuals.

Criminologists, on the other hand, are specifically concerned with the possibilities for true justice within the prevailing social order that defines a society. As a separate discipline concerned with crime, conflict, and control, criminology seeks to not only explain the relationship between society and justice, but to consolidate the need for social order with the principles of human rights. Order, according to the criminological perspective, that is achieved at the cost of violating the inalienable rights of any member of society is an order that must be both scrutinized and reformed.

Criminology, as a social focus, emerged with the publication of Cesare Beccaria's *Essay on Crimes and Punishment* in 1764. Beccaria's brief essay was written in the emerging period of the enlightenment when the "harsh and oppressive system of justice [much of it a remnant of a feudal social order] was subjected to the rational analysis of the men of the philosophical movement" (Sykes, 1978:8). Beccaria's goal was to humanize the law and the punishment for offenses. In his conclusion, Beccaria states (1963:99), "in order for punishment not to be, in every instance, an act of violence of one or many against a private citizen, it must be essentially public, prompt, necessary, the least possible in the given circumstance, proportionate to the crime, dictated by laws."

The Classical School of Criminology

Beccaria's ideas formed the major points of what is called the *Classical School of Criminology*. His ideas were thought of as forming the Classical School because it constituted the "first relatively adequate form or system of thinking in the area of criminology, just as Hebrew, Greek, and Latin are called the classical languages because they were the first to communicate adequately in modern abstract thinking" (Fox, 1976:35-36). This first step in criminology, made dramatically by Beccaria, formed the basis of later contributions. "It is not an exaggeration to regard Beccaria's work as being of primary importance in paving the way for penal reform for approximately the last two centuries" (Monachesi, 1972:49). Yet, the most important contribution of his work was "the foundation it laid for subsequent changes in criminal legislation" (Schafer, 1969:106). In other words, Beccaria's major contentions initiated or radically changed the thought on matters of crime and criminality.

Beccaria adopted the concept of the "social contract," which was beginning to be in vogue in the mid-1700s. "The concept held that an individual was bound to society only by his consent and therefore made society responsible to him as well as the reverse" (Reid, 1976:109). Beccaria felt that each person was required to give up only enough liberty to the society to make that society a viable entity. Following this train of thought, he saw laws as "the necessary conditions of the social contract, and punishments should exist only to defend the total sacrificed liberties against the usurpation of those liberties by other individuals" (Reid, 1976:109). This led to Beccaria's famous recommendation that the basis for all social actions must be the greatest happiness for the greatest number (Beccaria, 1963:11-13).

Another major point of Beccaria's argument was the contention that man operated under free will. It was believed that in every act man exercised a choice of alternatives and if he selected criminal behavior it was because he anticipated more pleasure and less pain from that choice. This is based on the principle of hedonism, the pleasure-pain principle: "Man choose those actions which would give pleasure and avoided those that would give pain" (Reid, 1976:109). Punishment was seen as a device which, when attached to a crime, would result in enough pain or anticipated pain to counteract the anticipated pleasure of the act. In order for this to be an effective philosophy, the laws must be written so that each person can read, understand, and interpret them, and the punishments must be fixed. This would require an end to capricious and arbitrary interpretations by judges. The philosophy of "let the punishment fit the crime" made the criminal law more impartial then it had been, and the judges became instruments of the law rather than rulers over it.

Jeremy Bentham, a contemporary of Beccaria, was another leader in the Classical School. He was an "armchair philosopher" who wrote on subjects that varied from the purpose of law to prison architecture. Because his thoughts were so radically different from the prevailing attitude of his time, Bentham has been labeled by one writer as "the greatest legal philosopher and reformer the world has ever seen" (Phillipson, 1923:234).

Beccaria and Bentham were of one mind in many areas. One of Bentham's most famous concepts advocated the greatest good must go to the greatest number. Within this concept is the theory of the *felicific calculus* (tending to cause happiness). "It assumed that man is a rational creature who will consciously choose pleasure and avoid pain. Therefore, a punishment must be assigned to each crime so that the pain would outweigh any pleasure derived from the commission of the crime" (Reid, 1976:110). The utility of criminal law and punishment was seen to be its deterrent effect.

It would be simplistic to imply that the thoughts and writings of Beccaria and Bentham were so original that they alone constitute the theoretical foundations for the Classical School of Criminology. In actuality, "the backgrounds of classical law involve the whole scope of preceding intellectual history, which had developed a theory of society, a philosophy of origins, and engendered a great deal of discussion about the relationship existing between the individual and the group" (Vold, 1958:15). Some of those who had the greatest influence on the emergence of the Classical School of Criminology, and ultimately on all criminological thought, were St. Thomas Aquinas (1224–1274), Martin Luther (1483–1546), Thomas Hobbes (1588–1679), John Locke (1632–1704), Voltaire (1694–1778), and Rousseau (1712–1778). These writers and thinkers contributed greatly to the philosophical environment of the late eighteenth century. Their formulation of the social contact led to its adoption in criminological thought.

Vernon Fox said of the Classical School (1976:38) that it,

[R]ejected the previously prevailing concepts of supernatural powers and the 'will of God' as the primary forces in human behavior, including criminal behavior, and substituted the free will of man and his intent. The consequent systemization of the discipline was built on the concept of free will; it eliminated human motives of revenge and substituted rational punishments that fit the seriousness of the crimes by causing rules to be determined and written into the law.

C. Ray Jeffery synthesized the Classical School into its two basic tenets (1956:666): "The Classical School (a) insists upon a clear-cut legal definition of that act which is to be punished as criminal and (b) fosters the idea of free will, that is, men commit crimes because of free choices of right and wrong." And finally, an excellent characterization of the Classical School was made by Vold (1958):

> It seems fair, therefore, to characterize the Classical School as administrative and legal criminology. Its great advantage was that it set up a scheme of procedure easy to administer. It made the judge only an instrument to apply the law, and the law undertook to prescribe an exact penalty for every crime and every degree thereof. Puzzling questions about the reasons for or (causes) of behavior, the uncertainties of motive and intent, the unequal consequences of an arbitrary rule, these were all deliberately ignored for the sake of administrative uniformity. This was the classical conception of justice—an exact scale of punishments for equal acts without reference to the nature of the individual involved and with no attention to the question of special circumstances under which the act came about.

The Positive School of Criminology

The *Positive School of Criminology* arose in the latter part of the nineteenth century in opposition to the harshness of the Classical School, as well as in response to the lack of concern for the causes of criminal behavior. The emergence of the Positive School "symbolized clearly that the era of faith was over and the scientific age had begun" (Schafer, 1969:123).

The shift in thinking during the century from the classical propositions and the birth of the Positive School was of such magnitude that one writer considers it an "intellectual revolution" (Vold, 1958:27). Science began to focus not on man's actions but on the creature "man." The answers came not from armchair philosophers but from scientists versed in "the logic and basic methodology of objective, empirical, and experimental science" (Vold, 1958:27). Darwin's *Descent of Man* was a true product of the times. Darwin proposed that man's "ancestors were other animals not so highly evolved as *Homo sapiens,* but nevertheless forming a continuous link with the earliest and simplest forms of life" (Vold, 1958:27). Data began to be collected for testing and verification in attempts to explain man's behavior based on what influenced him. "Man was beginning to appear to science as one of the many creatures, with no special link with divinity. Perhaps even more important, he was beginning to be understood, not as a self-determining creature who could do anything he made up his mind to do, but as a being whose conduct was 'determined' by his antecedents, biological and cultural" (Vold, 1958:28).

Cesare Lombroso, Enrico Ferri, and Raffaele Garofalo were major contributors to the intellectual atmosphere of evolution, biological and cultural, and determinism. They are known as the "Holy Three of Criminology" who "revolutionized the way of looking at the criminal and excited the world toward the scientific study of crime" (Schafer, 1969:123).

Cesare Lombroso (1835-1909), known as the father of positivistic criminology, was educated in medicine at the universities of Pavia and Genoa. He developed an interest in psychology and psychiatry while studying at the University of Vienna. As a young army physician, Lombroso measured the physical differences of some 3,000 soldiers. The data stimulated him to correlate psychic attitudes to physical characteristics. Later studies of the relationship between genius and insanity and genius and degeneration led him into the anthropometry of criminals. Lombroso's first major book, *L'Uomo Delinquente* (1876) or *The Criminal Man,* delineated his theory of the classification of criminals. The most unique portion of the theory concerned evolutionary atavism as an explanation of crime.

According to some writers (Barnes and Teeters, 1944:162; Schafer, 1969:125-126), Lombroso became acquainted with a powerful, energetic, and active man named Vilella, who was considered a dangerous criminal. When Vilella died, an autopsy was performed by Lombroso. "Upon opening Vilella's skull, Lombroso found an unusual depression, which he named *median occipital fossa,* and another depression, which he correlated with overdevelopment of the *vermis,* both known in the lower primates" (Schafer, 1969:125). The obvious conclusion, according to Lombroso, was that the criminal was an *atavus* or ancestor of modern man. He was a person with the ferocious and savage instincts of lower forms of animal life.

The atavistic criminal (or born criminal as Ferri labeled it) was not the only type of criminal according to Lombroso's classification scheme; the three major classifications of criminals were delineated as *born criminals, insane criminals,* and *criminaloids.* The last category defined those with no physical stigmata, or recognizable mental disorders, but who, under certain circumstances, would engage in criminal behavior. Vold summarizes the major points of Lombroso's work (1958:31):

1. He consistently emphasized the need for direct study of the individual, utilizing measurements and statistical methods in anthropological and in social and economic data.
2. He began with the basic assumption of the biological nature of human character and behavior:
   a. First conceived of the criminal as 'throwback' to a more 'primitive' type of brain structure, and therefore of behavior.
   b. Later modified this to include general degeneration or defectiveness.
   c. Never claimed that the 'born criminal' constituted more than 40 percent, probably less, only about a third of the total criminal population.
3. With successive years of study, discussion, and contact with critics, he modified his theory and method more and more to include all kinds of social, economic, and environmental data. Through it all, he always attempted to be:
   a. 'Objective' in method, often statistical.
   b. 'Positive' in the sense of deterministic.
   c. Faithful to the basic idea of cause as a 'chain of interrelated causes,' not the more familiar and popular doctrine of 'self-determinism' or human behavior, to say nothing on the demonistic or vital 'dynamic' doctrines often used to escape the implications of unpleasant facts in a deterministic system.

The importance of considering Lombroso, whose theories were proposed over a century ago, was well stated by Thorsten Sellin (1937:896–897): "Any scholar who succeeds in driving hundreds of fellow students to search for the truth, and whose ideas after half a century possess vitality, merits an honorable place in the history of thought."

Enrico Ferri (1856-1928) was a widely known, colorful student of Lombroso. At the age of twenty-one Ferri published a voluminous dissertation, *The Denial of Free Will and the Theory of Impunity,* in which he attacked the doctrine of free will. Ferri submitted a copy to Lombroso "who congratulated and encouraged him but did not find him 'positivist enough' " (Schafer, 1969:129). Ferri moved to the University of Turin where he became a pupil of Lombroso's and where he supplemented Lombroso's thinking as much as his was supplemented by Lombroso. Though greatly influenced by his mentor's ideas of biological causation, Ferri was more concerned with the impact of society upon human behavior.

Ferri developed and delineated his ideas on crime and criminality in two major publications: *L'omicidio-Suicidio* (Rome, 1884) and *La Sociologia Criminale* (Turin, 1884). In *The Homicide,* he specified the four classifications of criminal: *insane, born, occasional,* and *criminals by passion.* These classifications incorporated his ideas with those of Lombroso. But just as Lombroso had done, Ferri explained that these classifications were not the causes of criminal behavior, only indicators of that type of aggressive and vicious behavior. In his *Criminal Sociology,* Ferri maintained that crime was caused by a great number of factors which could be classified as *physical* (race, climate, location, season and temperature), *anthropological* (age, sex, organic and psychological conditions), and *social* (population density, customs, religion, economic and industrial conditions, and organization of government). He further specified social measures that would help to curb crime, such as free trade, abolition of monopolies, public savings banks, birth control, freedom of marriage and divorce, among others (Vold, 1958:33-34).

Active in politics, Ferri helped to initiate changes in the criminal law and penal policy of the time. His effort, through what was called the *Ferri Draft of 1921* (Fox,

1976:39), was such a radical change from the classical doctrine of previous years that it was found to be unacceptable to the Italian government.

Ferri sought to influence society to reject the concept of moral responsibility to explain human behavior and to replace it with the concept of social accountability:

> Ferri explained that just as cells, tissues, and organs have no independent biological existence in the body, so man has no sociological existence except as a member of a larger society. Without society there is no law, and without the law men cannot live together. The state and society have the right of self-preservation and the (natural necessity) to defend themselves. The state is unable to refrain from punishing the criminal in the defense of law and society (Schafer, 1969:130-131).

The final member of the trilogy in the founding of the Positive School was Raffaele Garofalo. Garofalo was educated in the law and groomed for the government service in Italy. He was a prolific writer and was greatly influenced by the works of Lombroso and Ferri; yet he found inadequacies in the theories of both.

Though he agreed with Lombroso and Ferri that the criminal was abnormal, he focused on the *psychic anomaly* rather than the physiological (Garofalo, 1914:79). He viewed the criminal, generally, as one who lacked the "proper development of the altruistic sensibility—a sensibility that has an organic basis and is not the result of environmental or economic factors."

Garofalo, as a true positivist, rejected the legal definition of crime. He was unique in that he replaced it with his own *natural crime* theory (Garofalo, 1914:4). By "natural," he meant "that which exists in a human society independently of the circumstances and exigencies of a given epoch or the particular views of the law maker ... (It describes) those acts which no civilized society can refuse to recognize as criminal and repress by means of punishment" (Garofalo, 1914:4-5). Gillin gives an excellent formulation of the "natural" definition of crime (1945:33-34):

> Crime is an immoral and harmful act that is regarded as criminal by public opinion because it is an injury to so much of the moral sense as is represented by one or the other of the elementary altruistic sentiments of probity and pity. Moreover, the injury must wound these sentiments not in their superior and finer degrees, but in the average measure in which they are possessed by a community—a measure which is indispensable for the adaptation of the individual to society.

As evident from the above quotation, Garofalo viewed criminality as falling in two categories: those affecting the sentiment of pity, such as crimes against the person; and those affecting the sentiment of probity, such as violent attacks on property. De Quirós maintains that this classification of crime, together with the definition of "natural," indicates that Garofalo rebuked positivism by embracing the notion of *natural morality*. "The old principles of morality and justice undergo so many amputations that the decalogue is reduced to only two commandments: *Thou Shalt Not Kill* (pity) and *Thou Shalt Not Steal* (probity)" (De Quiros, 1967:29).

Garofalo's classification of criminals was drastically different from those of Lombroso and Ferri. He classified criminals as *murderers,* that is, those who murder for the joy of the crime and possess no moral sense (Garofalo, 1914:376); *violent criminals,* those who kill or perform violent physical acts and who do so for egoistic satisfaction (Garofalo, 1914:385–389); *criminals deficient in probity* or respect for the property of others; and finally, the *lascivious criminal,* such as psychopaths and moral degenerates.

While the theories, ideas, and beliefs of the founders of the Positive School have been discussed at length, the Positive School itself transcends those theories. Indeed, it would be a mistake to link them too closely with the tenets of positivism because one could then say that positivism is the belief that criminals are atavistic or moral degenerates. While these theories are examples of early positivism, they have been presented only to indicate the radical change in ideology between the Classical School and Positive School.

In summary, the Positive School attacked the legal definition of crime espoused by the Classical School. "The positivist rejected the juridical concept of crime in favor of the sociologic notion of crime" (Jeffery, 1959:4). Garofalo substituted natural crime in the place of *Crimen Lege*. The Positive School views the criminal, not the crime, as the point of focus. The Positive School was based on the study of criminal behavior and scientific determinism. "Every act had a cause." "How and why do people commit crimes?" is the primary question positivists sought to answer. Finally, the Positive School surveyed, scrutinized, and tested problematic factors using the inductive method; empirical research was viewed as the only way of scientifically assessing the viability of a concept.

Although the methodologies utilized by the positivists was far from being perfected, their contributions to American criminology formed the foundation of American criminological thinking.

The Evolution of Criminological Theories

Criminology is and has always been a dynamic discipline. It is constantly evolving from one perspective to another and even from one discipline to another. The substantive area of criminology, beginning with Beccaria's *Of Crimes and Punishments* (1764), has been clothed in reform movements and even radicalism. "Radical" implies a considerable departure from the usual or traditional. New paradigms have always arisen to challenge the old. An examination of some current trends in sociology and criminology may help to exemplify the dynamics of the discipline and the diversity of the perspectives.

The crises, revolutions, and revelations of the last two decades have produced reverberations in many public and private structures. The academic area of social and behavioral sciences was one of the structures shaken by those crises. Gouldner stated in 1970 that academic sociology was "in the early stages of continuing crises" (1970:341). Chambliss used stronger terminology, observing that "sociology is in the throes of what Thomas Kuhn has called a period of 'paradigm revolution'—there is intensified criticism of the dominant theoretical paradigm and formulation of an alternative" (1973:1). This is not to imply that there would be a demise of sociology as a result of the crisis or revolution, but that sociology is undergoing a significant transformation. This transformation has been predicted to be in the direction of a *radical* or *conflict* perspective based on Marxism.

The crisis that sociology is experiencing became quite evident during the American Sociological Association Convention in 1968 when Martin Nicolaus delivered a speech that attacked the "sanctimonious sociological concepts of objective value-free science" (1968:154). His speech followed the address of the Secretary of Health, Education and Welfare, whom Nicolaus characterized as the "Secretary of Disease, Propaganda, and Scabbing" (1968:154):

> The department of which the man is head is more accurately described as the agency that watches over the inequitable distribution of preventable disease, over the funding of domestic propaganda and indoctrination, over the preservation of a cheap and docile reserve labor force to keep everybody else's wages down (1968:155).

He assailed sociologists by saying that their research and scientific study was focused on the 'down people' and the "professional palm of the sociologist is stretched toward the 'up people' " (Nicolaus, 1968:155).

Just as criminology developed out of the principles of sociology, it appears that it may also have contracted the coming "crisis" to which Gouldner referred. One writer even sees criminology as "both a reflection of and a force behind this revolution" (Chambliss, 1974:1). "In the United States we are presently witnessing and practicing a Radical Criminology, which has been developing in its latest form since the early 1960s and has begun to challenge the hegemonic domination of the field of liberal scholars" (Platt, 1974:2).

Annual increases in serious crime, overburdened prisons, and the apparent inability of corrections to correct, have caused many to question the ability of traditional criminology to effectively deal with the problem of crime. The result of this anomaly has been the awakening of the "era of radical writings" calling for a replacement of existing paradigms. Gibbons noted in 1974 that even though the Radical Criminology which was emerging at the time was immature and unsophisticated as a theory, it was certainly worthy of attention. Radical criminologists feel that it is time to closely inspect the "new criminology" in light of the "old criminology," the criminology steeped in both the classical and positive perspectives, in order to better identify that which may represent the impetus of a "paradigm revolution" (Kuhn, 1970). This is accomplished first by surveying that which precedes the "new criminology." But, as Meier points out (1977:8):

> I have argued that criminological theory represents a continuity with those views and perspectives that precede them. This continuity is one of the hallmarks of any scientific endeavor: intellectual innovations—whether they deal with methodological, conceptual, statistical, or theoretical issues—attempting to build upon, react to, or challenge those which came before. In this sense, there is nothing which is absolutely or uniquely new.

Sociology of Criminology

A major landmark in criminology and a significant work in the sociology of criminology perspective is C. Ray Jeffery's *The Structure of American Criminological Thinking* (1956). In this study Jeffery views the criminal law as the point of criminological structure which merits the most attention. He asserts that (1956:672):

> The sociology of criminal law should give us information concerning (1) the conditions under which behavior comes to be defined as criminal and (2) how legal norms intersect and are integrated with the norms of other institutional structures.

Jeffery's study is a critical analysis of criminology itself. He criticizes positivistic assumptions and specifically argues against studies of individual offenders in an effort to differentiate between the criminal and non-criminal. He maintains that, in fact, "the legal criterion is the only standard that differentiates the two groups" (1956:672).

Jeffery continued this train of thought when he addressed the historical development of criminology and examined the influence that early theoretical issues had in shaping modern criminology. He again stressed the need to examine the criminal law by stating (1959:19):

> The criminologist's attempt to separate criminology and criminal law, and his related attempt to derive criminality from the behavior of the criminal, *offer a major obstacle to a theory of crime.* More attention needs to be paid to the measuring of crime in terms of criminal law, social structure and social change. [Emphasis added.]

Another work in the sociology of criminology tradition is *The Criminologist: Crime and the Criminal,* edited by Charles E. Reasons (1974). In the preface, Reasons clearly states the concerns that are at the core of a sociology of criminology (1974:preface):

> Why has the criminologist emphasized certain types of crimes and criminals while neglecting others? What is the significance of interest groups in formulating, enforcing and administering laws? How is the criminologist to confront the nature and extent of political crime, corporate crime, state lawlessness, and the politization of prisoners? While I hardly claim to answer these questions, this book will address itself to these and other topics which will hopefully serve as a catalyst for further inquiry.

Again, the purpose of Reason's book is to confront criminology and criminologists with questions and propositions that cause discomfort but which certainly need to be addressed. "It would be easy for us to slip into small camps of believers who clutch tightly to different ideological positions" (Krishberg 1975:168). Yet, if criminology is to become a progressive, mature science, there must be a constant testing and analyzing of concepts. Through such critical analyses—a sociology of criminology—positions of proponents and opponents of various ideologies can be sharpened and clearly identified.

The Dominant Paradigm: Functional or Conflict?

Most writers agree that, within criminology today, there exists "a gigantic struggle between the previously dominant, *functional paradigm* and the emergent *conflict paradigm*" (Chambliss, 1976:1). It is perhaps a generality to dichotomize the criminological enterprise into two distinct categories, but each is treated separately to illustrate the magnitude and diversity of the struggle for paradigm dominance within the discipline itself.

Functionalism

Many classic writers in sociology and anthropology have equated society with the human organism. Herbert Spencer, in developing his theory of social evolution, saw the elements of growth in society as being "analogous to those of growth, struggle, and function in an animal" (Coser and Rosenberg, 1969:612). A function, for the social Darwinist, would be the contribution of the individual unit to the survival and growth of society. Durkheim further classified and popularized the word *function*. In *The Division of Labor in Society* (1964a), he proposed that function is like a biological element in an organism. A function, according to Durkheim, is that which is necessary for and assists in the preservation of the unit. Durkheim later asserted that the social system has needs which must be met repeatedly. A function could be considered a contribution to the maintenance of social life and society, such as social significance of ceremony and ritual (Durkheim, 1964).

Durkheim's organic analogy was continued and elaborated upon by A. R. Radcliffe-Brown. He maintained that "the concept of function applied to human societies is based on analogy between social life and organic life" (1956:178). Functionality was seen as a contribution to existence of the social structure:

> The continuity of structure is maintained by the process of social life which consists of the activities and interactions of the individual

human beings and of the organized groups into which they are united. The social life of the community is here defined as the *functioning* of the social structure. The *function* of any recurrent activity, such as the punishment of a crime, or a funeral ceremony, is the part it plays in the social life as a whole and therefore the contribution it makes to the maintenance of the structure's continuity (Radcliffe-Brown, 1956:189).

The American sociologist Robert Merton has modified Durkheim's views in order to stress the application of function to "observed consequences which make for the adaptation or adjustment of a given system, and *dysfunction,* those observed consequences which lessen adaptation or adjustment of the system" (Merton, 1968:105). In this analysis, function means a consequence rather than an emergent usefulness.

Durkheim was concerned with the function of crime in society. He saw its role to be that of establishing and maintaining the moral boundaries of the community (1949:102):

> Crime brings together upright consciences and concentrates them. We have only to notice what happens, particularly in a small town, when some moral scandal has just been committed. They stop each other on the street. They visit each other. They seek to come together to talk of the event and to wax indignant in common. From all the similar impressions which are exchanged, for all the temper that gets itself expressed, there emerges a unique temper . . . which is everybody's without being anybody's in particular. That is the public temper.

Thus, according to Durkheim's theory, crime is necessary.

The functional paradigm addresses areas of concern other than the "functions" of acts or behavior. On the causes of crime, the functional perspective views it as,

> behavior which occurs because one part of society (for example, the family, the schools, the division of labor, or the neighborhood) is not adequately instituting the society's agreed-upon customs into some of its members. The criminal law is explained as a reflection of the society's customary beliefs. Thus, both criminal behavior and criminal law have their roots in the customs of the society (Chambliss, 1974:4).

Value consensus is a central theme in functionalism, and the law is seen as a reflection of that consensus. Further, the state which is given the responsibility of enforcing the law is viewed as value neutral.

Functionalists view crime as normal and necessary. It is possible to determine what is criminal because it is possible to formulate the criminal law based on the collective conscience and the community's tolerance for deviancy. Those who commit crime do so because they have not been adequately socialized to the accepted values or they have been socialized to unaccepted values and customs. This explains the prevalence of members of the lower class in criminal behavior. "Criminal acts are more frequent among lower classes because the agencies of socialization (especially the family, but also the neighborhood, schools, other adult and peer groups) are less likely to work effectively" (Chambliss, 1974:9).

The functional perspective has guided the prominent means of treating offenders based on its assumptions as to the causes of crime. Treatment or rehabilitation is possible if corrections can neutralize the anti-social or extra-social elements within an individual and socialize him to the community's accepted behavior. This can be done through counseling, guidance, and therapy.

Conflict Perspective

The conflict perspective "suggests that society is an arena in which struggles over scarce commodities take place. The division of labor is felt to be the source of unequal distribution in a world of scarce resources" (Denisoff, 1974:297). Change rather than order is viewed as the essential ingredient of social life.

Karl Marx and Fredrick Engels constructed the basic elements of conflict theory (Marx and Engels, 1947:8–18; Marx, 1968:182–183). Denisoff (1974:298–299) synthesized and combined the general propositions of Marx's and Engels' theory into the following:

1. Life involves before everything else eating and drinking, a habitation, clothing ... (Marx and Engels, 1947:8).
2. The first historical act is ... the production of the means to satisfy these needs, the production of material life itself (Marx and Engels, 1947:16).
3. Men ... begin to distinguish themselves from animals as soon as they begin to produce their means of subsistence, a step which is conditioned by their physical organization ... (through this) ... men are indirectly producing material life (Marx and Engels, 1947:7).
4. ... in the social productions of their life, men enter into definite relations (the division of labor) that are indispensable and independent of their will, relations of production which correspond to a definite state of development of their material productive forces (Marx, 1968:182).
5. The sum total of these relations of production constitutes the economic structure of society, the real foundation, on which rises a legal and political superstructure and to which correspond definite forms of social consciousness (Marx, 1968:182).
6. The second fundamental point is that as soon as a need is satisfied ... new needs are made ... (Marx and Engels, 1947:17).
7. The third circumstance which, from the very first, enters into historical developments is that men, who daily remake their own life, mean to make other men, to propagate their kind ... (Marx and Engels, 1947:17).
8. The production of life, both of one's own in labour and of fresh life in progression, now appears as a double relationship: on the one hand as a natural, on the other hand a social relationship (Marx and Engels, 1947:18).
9. ... it is quite obvious from the start that there exists a materialistic connection of men with one another, which is determined by their needs and their mode of production and which is as old as men themselves (Marx and Engels, 1947:18).
10. Each new productive force ... brings about a further development of the division of labour (Marx and Engels, 1947:8).
11. The various stages of development in the division of labour are just so many forms of ownership (Marx and Engels, 1947:9).
12. The production of ideas, of conceptions, of consciousness, is at first directly interwoven with material activity ... (Marx and Engels, 1947:13-14).
13. At a certain stage of their development, the material productive forces of society come into conflict with the existing relations of production.... Then begins an epoch of social revolutions (Marx, 1968:182).

14. With the change of economic foundation, the entire immense superstructure is more or less rapidly transformed (Marx, 1968:182-183).

So, according to Marx, the most basic requirements of life—food, shelter, and clothing—are met through the manipulation of the environment—labor. Man, as distinguished from animals, is constantly producing in order to survive. For Marx, this indicated that the nexus of existence is economic and that all other structures—superstructures—are both built upon and supportive of the economic substructure. When people cease to regard the institutions of politics, religion, and government—superstructures—as sacred, the struggle between the economically elite and the economically deprived begins. The result is social change.

Marxist social conflict provided a point from which many theories began. Ralf Dahrendorf altered Marx's conflict theory in several areas (1959). Marx saw conflict as being rooted in class differences; yet Dahrendorf viewed it as a problem of unequal authority. Marx's propositions focused on internal conflict while Dahrendorf saw most conflict coming from external sources. Finally, Dahrendorf held that many conflicts are not capable of resolution and a compromise must be sought. Marx saw no room for compromise.

Focusing on the area of deviant behavior, the conflict perspective holds that criminality is "behavior that exploits vulnerable others, whether or not it is defined as crime in legal formulas or practice" (Turk, 1977:216). Though this represents an extreme view (which will be expanded later), generally the criminal law is seen as the tool of the ruling class to provide the state, synonymous with the ruling class, with the coercive force to repress the ruled. For conflict theorists, crime is "concentrated in the lower classes because the ruling class can see that only acts which grow out of lower class life are defined as criminal" (Chambliss, 1974:9). Perhaps the central theme is that "acts are defined as criminal because it is in the interests of the ruling class to so define them. . . . The single most important force behind criminal law creation is doubtless the economic interest and political power of those social classes which either (1) own or control the resources of the society or (2) occupy positions of authority in the state bureaucracies" (Chambliss, 1974:9–11).

2. Early Criminological Theories

Biological Theories

In the preceding discussion of the Positive School of Criminology, the theories of Lombroso, Ferri, and Garofalo were presented to exemplify the philosophical tenets of that school of thought. It was pointed out that the Positive School stood for more than the substantive theories of the "Holy Three." Their theoretical orientation "was for the most part substantively biological. Their approach to the study of crime was positivistic in that they utilized or attempted to utilize the point of view and methodology of the natural sciences" (Quinney, 1970:57–58). Their theories, however, are only a small representation of the many perspectives stemming from the physiological or biological explanations of criminal behavior.

Studying the physical and biological characteristics of the criminal is a traditional approach in criminology. As an emerging field whose proponents adhered to the positivistic notion of the scientific method, biological and physiological differences formed an attractive milieu in which to study the causes of crime. It seemed both logical and scientific, perhaps in a simplistic way, to believe that people behave differently because they are structurally different. "All biological explanations rest on the basic logic that *structure determines function*" (Vold, 1959:43). It is understandable that a new discipline within the social and behavioral sciences would rally around the methodologically and philosophically simple concept of biological reductionism or the theory that behavior can be reduced from philosophical, sociological explanations to the concept of biological determinism. "Man's social organization has developed as a result of his biological evolution—hence, social evolution is subsequent to, but essentially parallel with, and presumably a product of, biological evolution (Vold, 1958:10).

J. Baptiste della Porte (1535-1615) has been referred to as the "first criminologist." He studied the character of criminals with the hope of developing a relationship between physical characteristics and the type of crime the person had committed. For example, della Porte determined that thieves could be identified by their "small ears, bushy eyebrows, small nose, mobile eyes, sharp vision, open and large lips, and long slender fingers" (della Porte, 1586 in Schafer, 1969:113).

Physiognomy became an accepted field of study during the time of Cesare Beccaria. Johan Caspar Lavater (1741-1801) published a four-volume work on physiognomy—the determination of character based on facial features—entitled *Physiognomical Fragments* in 1775. In the books, Lavater showed the relationship of behavior or character with facial "fragments" such as the nose, eyes, beard, ears, and chin. Lavater's ideas reflect the basic underpinnings of the more established views set forth in the science of "phrenology."

The practice of phrenology holds that the "localization of brain function can be found by determining what areas (of the brain) have been developed by use or by heredity and by 'reading' the bumps on (the) head" (Fox, 1976:401). Franz Joseph Gall is credited for having developed the doctrines of phrenology. For almost thirty years, beginning in 1791, Gall published materials indicating the relationships between skull conformation and the characteristics of individuals. The publication of the final restatement of his position (Gall, 1825) ended Gall's controversial and tremendously opposed efforts.

One of Gall's students, John Gaspar Spurzheim (1776-1832), did much to further the work initiated by Gall.

Spurzheim, a noted writer and speaker of his time, gave lectures in England and America which were instrumental in clarifying and spreading the concepts he and Gall had formulated. The specific tenets of his theory of phrenology were:

> The exterior of the skull conforms to the shape of the brain; the so-called mind (or brain) consists of several faculties or functions; and these faculties are related to specific areas of the brain and skull and therefore bumps on the skull are indicators of the (organs) of specific faculties. ... Gall found twenty-seven faculties or functions of the brain, and Spurzheim extended this list to thirty-five.

In America, the leading proponent of phrenology was Charles Caldwell (1772–1853), who published the first American text on the subject (1824). Vold (1958:46–47) discusses the points within Caldwell's theory that made it unique:

> Caldwell elaborated the theory with a further assumption of the hierarchical relation between propensities, sentiments, and intellectual faculties. Thus the sentiments control the propensities, and aided by the *will* the intellectual faculties enlighten, direct, and govern the whole. If a person should have the organ of covetousness strongly developed but not controlled by sentiments or will or intellect, the result would be dishonesty and theft.

Although phrenology was far from scientific in the true sense, its deterministic qualities and its convenient categories made it popular. Vold relates (1958:47–49) that these "medicine men," the phrenologists, were highly sought after as speakers, teachers, and as "scientific read[ers] of character." The popularity of phrenology is illustrated as well by the fact that the Eastern State Penitentiary of Pennsylvania used the categories supplied by phrenologists for nearly seventy years. With its popularity, however, came criticisms by the scientific community. These criticisms keyed on the fact that the basic assumptions made by phrenologists were purely hypothetical. Because phrenology could not counter the criticism with verifiable data, it was soon rejected as a viable means to study criminal behavior.

Cesare Lombroso's theory of degeneracy in which physical

stigmata were indicators of criminality has already been discussed. His study of physical anomalies, while within the realm of scientific methodology, was statistically questionable. Yet other studies along the same vein were more exact and carefully prepared. Such a study was conducted by Charles Goring and his group of investigators in England. The study began in 1901 and covered a period of eight years. Because the study was so extensive and statistical manipulations so intricate and involved, the results were not published until 1913 under the now famous title *The English Convict* (Goring, 1913). The study involved the examination and measurement of 3000 English convicts and a large group of noncriminal Englishmen. Part of Goring's study included testing Lombroso's assertations. Lombroso had maintained that the criminal, when compared to the general population, would be seen to have certain physical anomalies or defects. Goring intended to test this proposition by comparing criminals—all recidivists—to a group of noncriminals—university students of Oxford and Cambridge, hospital patients, and the officers and men of the Royal Engineers of the British Army.

Although Goring used exemplary care in the methodology of his study, the facts failed to support Lombroso's studies. Goring found no anomalies among the convicts with regard to facial features, head weight, width or circumference, protrusions or differences in symmetry. Goring also tested the possibility that there were differences in the characteristics of different types of criminals, such as burglars, forgers, and thieves. He found that the physical characteristics were no different from one type or another (Goring, 1913:196-214). The only significant differences Goring found were that the criminals were shorter than noncriminals and they weighed less than noncriminals. These differences were interpreted by Goring to be indicative of hereditary inferiority, which he believed to be the basis for deviant behavior (Goring, 1913:200).

For over twenty-five years Goring's conclusion that "there

is no such thing as a physical type" stood unchallenged. However, in 1939 a Harvard anthropologist, Ernest A. Hooton, published a twelve-year study which, according to Hooton, showed persuasively that the criminal is organically inferior. The study (Hooton, 1939) had a total sample size of over 17,000 persons. The criminal group contained 13,873 persons incarcerated in jails and prisons, and 3,203 sane and insane noncriminals (Hooton, 1939: Vol. I, 309).

Some of Hooton's conclusions are indicative of his ideology. He maintained criminals were "inferior" to noncriminals in nearly all body measurements (Hooton, 1939:229). He further maintained that inferiority is due to heredity, and physical inferiority is an indication of mental inferiority (Hooton, 1939:306-308).

A major portion of Hooton's study dealt with comparisons of criminals by type of offense. In this area he focused on the general somatotype of the offender and concluded that tall, thin men are disposed to be murderers and robbers, undersized men are thieves and burglars, and short, heavy men tend to commit sex crimes (Hooton, 1931:376-378).

The response to Hooton's work was largely unfavorable. His sample was not representative of the population in either the criminal group or the noncriminal group. There was no evidence that the "inferiority" which he measured was inherited. Schafer notes (1969:187) that Robert Merton and Ashley Montagu (1940:384-408) found that Hooton's "control group shows more similarity to anthropoid apes than to his criminal population."

At about the same time that Hooton was collecting his data, the German psychiatrist Ernest Kretschmer (1888-1964) was enumerating his classification of men by physical characteristics and their corresponding temperament (Kretschmer, 1925). He, following other typologists concerned with mental disorders, classified men psychologically as manic depressive and schizophrene. The body types were labeled as *asthenic* and *athletic* types, both of whom are predominately *schizophrenes,* and *pyknics,* who tend to be *manic depressives*. In a later publication (1955:331–357), Kretschmer stated that athletic types seem to be connected with crimes of violence, asthenic types with larceny or fraud, and pyknics with crimes of deception. Kretschmer's work had a great deal of influence on the work of William H. Sheldon.

Sheldon specifically studied the relationship between the shape of the body and delinquency (Sheldon, 1949). Sheldon examined 200 male youths who had been, between 1939 and 1949, in the Hayden Goodwill Inn, a type of rehabilitation home in Boston. He classified them as to physique and temperament. Vold produced a schematic arrangement (1958:71) by synthesizing the material presented by Sheldon (1949:14–30).

Physique	Temperament
1. Endomorphic: relatively great development of digestive viscera; tendency to put on fat; soft roundness through various regions of the body; short, tapering limbs; small bones, soft, smooth, velvety skin.	1. Viscerotonic: general relaxation of body; a comfortable person; loves soft luxury; a 'softie' but still essentially an extrovert.
2. Mesomorphic: relative predominance of muscles, bone, and the motor-organs of the body; large trunk; heavy chest; large wrists and hands; if 'lean,' a hard rectangularity of outline; if 'not lean,' they filled out heavily.	2. Somotonic: active, dynamic, person; walks, talks, gestures assertively; behaves aggressively.
3. Ectomorphic: relative predominance of skin and its appendages which includes the nervous system; lean, fragile, delicate body; small face, sharp hose, fine hair; relatively little body mass and relatively great surface area.	3. Cerebrontonic: an introvert; full of functional complaints, allergies, skin troubles, chronic fatigue, insomnia; sensitive to noise and distractions; shrinks from crowds.

Sheldon related the constitutional factors—body type—with the temperamental factors which he related to propensities to commit crime.

Medical and psychiatric advances have recently produced many explanations of abnormal behavior. Some of the explanations have been made by observing the results of medical treatment. The areas of psychosurgery, castration, psychopharmacology, and stereotactic treatment have all been proposed as means of treating those who exhibit criminal, deviant, or aggressive behavior. The value of these means of treatment may be obvious to medical practitioners, but criminologists are not likely to rally around such extreme and often irreversible measures.

The theories and theorists of the positivists in the biological milieu have been helpful to criminology only in so far as they transgressed theories of crime based on metaphysical musings. The greatest contribution of the biological theorists is the development of the scientific perspective of criminology and the delineation of that which is problematic—the causes of criminal behavior. Specifically, the biological theorists constructed the framework that stressed the importance of focusing on the individual as an answer to deviant behavior. In this vein, the psychological theories of other positivists gained popularity.

Psychological Theories

In keeping with the positivistic tradition, theories that concentrated on the mind of the offender as the cause of his actions became popular in the early twentieth century. The emerging field of criminology viewed the psychological explanations as being more abstract than those of biological determinism. This attribute, however, was viewed positively, and criminologists regarded psychological theories of crime as being more philosophically sound than those offered by biological determinists.

Some of the earliest attempts to explain behavior concentrated on mental anomalies. When stone-age men believed that a person was possessed of devils, the remedy was a process called "trephining," which was cutting a hole in the skull of the person to allow the evil spirit to escape. Exorcism was the popular method of removing evil spirits during the medieval times. During the fifteenth century it was believed that some possessed people were working with the devil of their own free will, which was promptly labeled witchcraft. Since the "witchcraft" was of the person's own free will, it was readily agreed that he deserved to be punished for this wicked collusion and that the punishment should be severe. This view was consistent with that of the Classical School, which formed soon after this period.

As was discussed in an earlier section, the view that many abnormalities or anomalies were biologically determined began in the eighteenth century. By the twentieth century it was being argued that psychological problems could cause mental illness. This contention had obvious implications for the field of criminology.

Psychiatry, the area of medicine that deals specifically with mental problems, includes psychology. For purposes of this discussion, the two will be combined for a general discussion of the theories of criminal behavior that concentrate on mental anomalies.

William Healy was one of the first physicians to view delinquency as caused by anything other than biological deficiencies. He examined psychiatric and neurological characteristics in addition to the physical characteristics and environmental characteristics of the individuals. His objective was to formulate methods of treatment, and he maintained that "one can most surely and safely arrive at remedial measures through investigation of the mental factors" (Healy, 1915:31). He and his wife, a psychologist, in an effort to develop a body of research that would be empirically valid, conducted numerous case studies. They were interested in the true causes behind delinquent behavior.

Actually, Healy was simply continuing the work of others in psychiatry who had begun to attribute crime to mental deficiencies. Almost 100 years before Healy, English law judges ruled on a case in which a man named Daniel M'Naghten felt that Sir Robert Peel should be executed in the best interests of the country. When he attempted to carry out this "altruistic" chore, he mistakenly killed Peel's secretary. The court ruled that M'Naghten could not be considered guilty because he was insane. In 1843 a legal definition of insanity was formulated in regard to the case:

> To establish a defense of insanity, it must be clearly proved that, at the time of committing the act, the party accused was labouring under such a defect of reason, from disease of the mind, as not to know the nature and quality of the act he was doing; or, if he did know it, that he did not know it was wrong (M'Naghten, 1843:200).

Isaac Ray proposed more than fifty years before Healy that medical evidence was available that indicated that some cannot resist committing crimes even though they are "fully conscious of their nature and consequences" (Ray, 1885:263).

Healy's contributions were also based on certain accomplishments in the field of psychiatry and mental testing. In 1905 Alfred Binet and Theodore Simon constructed a test scale measuring a person's "intelligence quotient," which is the ratio of the mental age of the person as indicated by his test score, multiplied by 100, and divided by his chronological age. This Binet-Simon intelligence scale has been revised many times and is now called the Stanford-Binet test.

Sigmund Freud (1856–1939) attempted to provide a theory for the explanation of all behavior, including deviant or criminal behavior. Central to his theory was the idea that there exists mental conflict due to incompatible elements of the personality. Unacceptable or unpleasant portions of this conflict are repressed into the unconscious and kept there by a *censor,* "a term used to describe the capacity to force unity and harmony into the obvious and conscious personality by repressing the undesirable elements into the unconscious" (Vold, 1958:117).

Early Freudian formulations (1920) saw the nature of the

individual as being conflict. This conflict was centered in the *libido,* the energy of force that controls the individual drives, urges, and impulses. Later discussion (1927) identified three basic elements of the personality that must be in balance. The *id* is that part of the unconscious which is the reservoir of biological and psychological drives and urges. This includes the *libido*—predominantly, the sexual drives. The *superego* is that part of the unconscious which involves self-criticism and conscience. It is the superego based on socialized and internalized norms that controls the individual. The conscious part of the personality of which the individual is aware is the *ego*. This ego acts as a "referee" between the id and the superego. When unacceptable conflicts between the id and the superego take place, the ego, as a defense mechanism, represses them into the unconscious. The conflicts may later emerge in other forms such as complexes or criminal behavior. So, according to Freudian theory, crime is a "substitute expression of repressed personality experiences" (Schafer, 1976:65). The treatment for this type of behavior is the release of repressed conflicts from the unconscious through various means.

William Healy has been said to be the author of the shift in criminology from biological to psychological concerns in criminal behavior, but, based on the influence of others who preceded him, it might be more appropriate to state that he was one of the first to use the Freudian view of dynamic psychiatry to examine deviant behavior. In 1936 Healy and August Bronner, his wife, released their book *New Light on Delinquency and Its Treatment,* which they claimed showed unquestionably the relationship of emotional disturbances with delinquency. They did stipulate that other environmental factors had an influence on criminality.

In 1950 Healy's ideas were reflected in a study constructed by Sheldon and Eleanor Glueck. In this study carefully controlled comparisons of 500 delinquent boys and 500 nondelinquent boys were made. The groups were matched with respect to age, intelligence, natural origins, and residence in underprivileged neighborhoods. Personality inventories were administered, particularly the Rorschach *Ink Blot Test*. The results of the comparison of mental pathology are presented in Table 1 (Glueck, 1950:239).

The findings represent a confusing menagerie of traits that involves mental, physical, and social factors in the tendencies toward delinquency.

Similarly, David Abrahamsen, a psychiatrist, viewed everyone as having a tendency to commit crime; therefore, that which is problematic is the question of what stimulates the criminal impulse. He developed the formula:

$$C = \frac{T + S}{R}$$

C indicates "Crime," T stands for "Tendencies," R for "Resistances" to impulses, and S for "Situation" (Abrahamsen, 1960:37). This was an extension of previous work in the multiplicity-of-factors approach which included mental or psychological anomalies.

The development of psychological theories of criminal behavior began with a total explanation focusing on mental anomalies. These theories evolved into the *multiplicity-of-factors* approach which included, to a great degree, sociological and ecological circumstances of the delinquent.

Sociological Theories

Sociological theories are developed to explain normal and abnormal behavior; yet in many cases these theories do not allow rigorous retesting and recomputation as is done in the fields of biology and even psychology. One writer states that "much of what is labeled sociological theory is, in reality, only a loose clustering of implicit assumptions, inadequately defined concepts, and a few vague and logically disconnected propositions" (Turner, 1974:9). In spite of this, the multiplicity-of-factors approach professed by psychologists indicates that a person's social environment merits attention as perhaps one of the primary keys to the question of criminality.

A discussion of sociological theories in criminology from a strict chronological point of view would be very confusing because of the "leap-frog" method by which some theories came into prominence. The approach utilized in this study is the presentation of four logical groupings of theories: *control theories, strain theories, cultural deviance theories,* and *symbolic interaction theories.*

Control Theory

"Control theories assume that delinquent acts result when an individual's bond to society is weak or broken" (Hirschi, 1969:16). In a control theory, order and conformity to rules are problematic. In other words, control theories do not focus on the question of why some deviate from society's norms and others do not. Man is assumed to be amoral; therefore, control theory is concerned with what causes man to conform. Control theories are based on examining the contradictions of man's nature (amoral) and the necessity for social order.

The rationale of the control theorist follows Cohens' statement (1959:463): "A theory of deviant behavior must not only account for the occurrence of deviant behavior, it must also account for its failure to occur . . . the explanation of one necessarily implies the explanation of the other." Stinchcombe worded the idea more succinctly (1964:4): "The explanation of deviance and conformity are interchangeable." The pure control theorist might say "what needs to be explained, then, is not so much why we behave badly as how we can be induced to behave well" (Nettler, 1974:216). The theories that focus on this element of control will be the first to be reviewed.

Emile Durkheim (1964) believed that one of the most important aspects of a society is that of social solidarity, which represents a collective conscience. He saw the normal condition of society as being one in which individuals were tightly bound to one another. A crime, then, is that which would shock the collective conscience of a community. This collective conscience reflects society acting with each person to control or inhibit deviance.

Along these same lines, Albert Reiss (1951) discussed personal control as a result of attachment to others. This attachment of the individual to others assists in and insists upon the internalization of the norms of society or at least the norms of those with whom the individual is attached. In Reiss' study of the characteristics of working-class boys in Chicago (1952), the subjects, all male probationers of the juvenile court, were classified as to psychological types. Of the 1110 subjects, 65% were identified as relatively integrated delinquents and 12% were seen as having defective superego controls. As to the latter category, Reiss commented that "delinquents with markedly defective superego controls have not internalized the social-conforming controls of middle-class society and experience little sense of guilt over their delinquent acts. Typically they identify with an adolescent peer culture which rejects these norms" (Reiss, 1952:710-711). Therefore, it is the lack of normative controls that allows a person to break the bonds of societal expectations.

TABLE 1

Pathology	Delinquents	Non Delinquents	Difference
No Conspicuous Pathology	48.6%	55.7%	−7.1%
Asocial, "Primative," Poorly Adjusted, Unstable	16.9%	5.9%	11.0%
Neuroticism	24.6%	35.8%	−11.2%
Psychopathy	7.3%	.4%	6.9%
Organic Disturbances	.8%	.2%	.6%
Psychotic Trends	.4%	1.6%	−1.2%
Undifferentiated Pathology	1.4%	.4%	1.0%

This study included many more comparisons and analyses and the conclusion was that:

> A meaningful pattern does tend to emerge from the interweaving of separately spun strands; on the whole, delinquents are more extroverted, vivacious, impulsive, and less self-controlled than the nondelinquent. They are more hostile, resentful, defiant, suspicious and destructive. They are less fearful of failure or defeat than the nondelinquents. They are less concerned about meeting conventional expectations, and are more socially assertive. To a greater extent than the control group, they express feelings of not being recognized or appreciated (Glueck, 1950:275).

Gresham Sykes and David Matza (1957) developed a theory of delinquency which held that a person was able to be controlled due to the existence of moral obstacles and became delinquent only when these obstacles could be neutralized. Fox, in discussing the techniques of neutralization (1976:139), says "the delinquent's value system is not consistently oppositional to the dominant social order; however, he is able to situationally qualify behavioral norms in which he believes and this allows him to engage in disapproved behavior." The techniques used to rationalize the "guilt" or conscience of the delinquent are (Sykes, 1957:664–670):

1. Denial of responsibility—the delinquent is a victim of circumstances
2. Denial of injury—no one was hurt by the crime
3. Denial of the victim—injury was not wrong, given the situation in which it took place
4. Condemnation of the condemner—delinquent displaces the guilt by calling condemners hypocrites or criminals themselves
5. Appeal to higher loyalties—the smaller group demands more loyalty and sacrifice than the larger group—the society.

The delinquent, in other words, sees these forms of justification as valid, but this view is not shared by the law or society.

Walter Reckless formulated what is considered one of the classic versions of control theory. His contention, called *containment theory* (1973), holds that there are certain sources of controls or means of containment that help the individual to conform. These sources of control are referred to as inner control systems and outer control systems. External or outer control forces include social pressures, poverty, deprivation, conflict, minority-group status, opportunity structures, religion, peer pressure, training in roles, affiliation with a community, and standards of conduct. These forces may be positive, in which case they contain or control the individual so that he does not engage in crime, or they may be negative and "push" the person toward delinquency. The inner control forces include self-concept, self-control, ego strength, superego development, tolerance for frustration, and sense of responsibility. These forces can also be seen as favoring delinquency or conformity.

Outer control systems, according to Reckless, are social pressures to conform. As stated previously, these pressures are exerted by peers, family, religion—all institutions that seek to develop a sense of belonging. Inner containment or self-control is necessary, however, because no society can exist secure in the belief that external social pressures will cause everyone to conform. Nettler maintains (1974:219) that "all socialization aims implicitly, if not explicitly, at the development of self-control. The agent of such control is commonly called 'conscience.' " In Reckless' schema this inner control is the result of a moral training that produces five indicators of its presence: (1) a healthy self-concept; (2) goal-directedness; (3) a realistic level of aspiration; (4) the ability to tolerate frustration; and (5) an identification with lawful norms. The degree of development of each of these indicators points to the likelihood of deviance or conformity.

Hirschi developed a *control theory of delinquency* (1969:16–34) that embraced the concept that conformity is the result of the bond of the individual to society (1969:16). This bond is the sociological counterpart of the superego or conscience; this attachment is seen as *commitment,* which "is the counterpart of the ego or common sense" (Hirschi, 1969:20); *involvement* or the engrossment in activities either conventional or nonconventional; and the *belief* in a common value system within society. Hirschi examines the relationship between these attachments and the external elements of society, such as parents, schools, conventional activities, and other sociological factors (Hirschi, 1969:23). He concluded that "the values in question are available to all members of American society more or less equally; they are accepted or rejected to the extent they are consistent or inconsistent with one's realistic position in that society" (Hirschi, 1969:230).

Control theory presumes that even though we are born as *Homo sapiens,* we become human beings only through socialization. It further specifies what elements of socialization or what indices of socialization are present in the conformist; therefore, if the elements or indices are weakened, the individual may become deviant.

Strain Theory

The assumption that forms the basis of strain theory is that man is a moral animal who innately desires to conform (Hirschi, 1969:5). The question strain theorists attempt to answer is "what is the cause of nonconformity?" According to strain theories, if individuals fail to conform, the cause must be due to some pressure or strain. "In the classic strain theories, this pressure is provided by legitimate desires" (Hirschi, 1969:5).

Strain theorists are concerned with determining the extraordinary motivation for deviant behavior or with identifying the extraordinary motivation that leads to the subculture, which then leads to deviant behavior. There is believed to be a uniform moral influence in society that transmits societal expectations to everyone. Deviance is not a normal phenomenon but requires an exceptional stress or strain to account for it. This stress is sometimes provided by a real or perceived discrepancy in societal expectations and the individual's situation.

Durkheim, in his study of suicide, discussed, among other

types, the concept of *anomique suicide.* Anomie is derived from the Greek word meaning lawlessness. Durkheim uses the term to mean a lack of regulation or normlessness. Anomique suicide is a consequence of society's reduced moral regulation and the absence of social cohesion, and solidarity. Anomie occurs when an individual can no longer identify with normative standards of conduct or beliefs. This weakened sense of social solidarity leads to anxieties that are often released through criminal behavior.

As early as 1938 Robert Merton took the concept of anomie and applied it to the question of deviancy. He constructed an elaborate theory aimed at the discrepancy between culturally defined goals and socially accepted means (1957). According to Merton's theory, there are two common characteristics of all social structures. The first is the *establishment of goals,* objectives that each member of the society should strive for. The second social characteristic is *the provision of means* to reach those goals. Some societies place emphasis on the goals, others on the means, but as long as individuals accept the culturally defined goals and the socially approved means, there is conforming behavior. When one or the other is rejected, the result is nonconforming behavior.

After examining the patterns of behavior in American society, Merton constructed a method of classifying the modes of adaptation to the goals and the means. He labelled behavior by its acceptance or rejection of the goals and the means approved by society.

Conformity is the adaptation whereby the individual accepts the culturally defined goals and uses the approved means to strive for those goals. *Innovation* describes the adaptation of accepting socially approved goals but rejecting the means of attaining those goals. This form of adaptation leads to deviant behavior. If society establishes goals of two cars and a color television in every home, yet the traditional means for attaining the goals—hard work, good job—are rejected for one reason or another, an individual will innovate and find other means for reaching these goals. If the individual feels pressured to achieve certain goals set forth by society, yet feels that legitimate means are blocked, the inevitable result is deviant behavior. "In this setting, a cardinal American virtue, 'ambition,' promotes a cardinal American vice, 'deviant behavior'" (Merton, 1968:200).

This explanation is particularly useful in studying crime in poverty areas. Merton stipulates that poverty in itself does not cause crime, but "when poverty and associated disadvantages in competing for the culture values approved for *all* members of the society are linked with a cultural emphasis on pecuniary success as a dominant goal, high rates of criminal behavior are the normal outcome" (Merton, 1968:201).

The next mode of adaptation is *ritualism*. In this form of adaptation, cultural goals are rejected but the means are accepted. This mode may not represent real deviant behavior but "it clearly represents a departure from the cultural mode in which men are obliged to strive actively, preferably through institutionalized procedures, to move onward and upward in the social hierarchy" (Merton, 1968:204). In this type of adaptation, it might not be clear to the individual as to *why* he is doing something, such as working diligently or going to church, but he knows that it is the accepted thing to do. As one writer said, the individual has lost sight of the reasons for doing things (Reid, 1976:179). This disorientation may lead to a final rejection of both social goals and means.

Retreatism, the next mode of adaptation, involves the conscious rejection of social goals and means, and the individual, in effect, becomes an alien of society. Merton suggests that some conformists who have repeatedly failed to achieve social goals through accepted means are often unable to replace the legitimate means with deviant means. The presence of the goals and the ineffectualness of approved means represent a source of internal conflict; thus the individual seeks to escape. When "the escape is complete, the conflict is eliminated and the individual is disassociated" (Merton, 1968:208). People who follow this mode of adaptation are severely criticized by society because they are nonproductive. Vagabonds, vagrants, drunkards, drug addicts and psychotics are examples of individuals who have retreated into an alien world.

Rebellion, the last mode of adaptation discussed here, "leads people outside the social structure to envisage and try to establish a modified social struggle" (Fox, 1976:118). In this type of adaptation, the goals and means are rejected and replaced with others in attempts to establish a new social order. Rebellion reflects a desire to adapt to an alternative mode of existence.

Albert Cohen followed the same path of examination and explanation as Merton. He looked specifically at the development of delinquent subculture (Cohen, 1955). Cohen says that lower-class children are measured by the "middle-class measuring rod," which means that the lower-class child accepts the goals of the middle class and of society but does not have the means to accomplish the goals. The lower-class child within a middle-class society is typically judged according to middle-class standards. "He [the lower-class child] has been socialized to live for today and to place more value on physical aggression than is characteristic of the middle class" (Reid, 1976:181). The lower-class child experiences confusion because of the conflict between the "is" and the "ought," between the reality of his life and what he has been told should be. The lower-class child who is confused by unrealistic expectations can easily be pressured into a subculture that is characterized by short-run hedonism and group autonomy, and whose activities are non-utilitarian, malicious, and negativistic. Cohen's theory proposes that anomie, the strain created from the denial of access to status in society, results in the creation of a subculture where status can be gained apart from middle-class standards.

Richard Cloward and Lloyd Ohlin (1961) "brought anomie into an *opportunity theory;* they felt that the tension between recommended goals and available means presents a strain that the individual must handle in some way, and some go in the direction of crime and delinquency by using illegitimate means to achieve recommended goals" (Fox, 1976:121). Just as Cohen did, they examined the disparity between society's goals or aspirations and the available means of opportunity. The opportunity structures can be legitimate or illegitimate. If one is available and the other blocked, the response is obvious. Given limited access to success, that is, attaining goals by legitimate means, "the nature of the delinquent response that may result will vary according to the availability of various illegitimate means" (Cloward and Ohlin, 1961:150).

Subcultures have been identified by such studies as being *criminal, conflict,* or *retreatist.* Criminal subcultures or gangs see the acquisition of money and valuables as the proper opportunity structure. "The child has an opportunity to actually perform illegitimate roles because such activity finds support in his immediate neighborhood milieu. The rewards—monetary and other—of successful learning and performance are immediate and gratifying at each age level" (Cloward and Ohlin, 1961:164–165). The environment supports criminal activity tacitly, if not otherwise, so that the criminal opportunity structure is seen to be the most appropriate. The conflict subculture is the second type identified by Cloward and Ohlin. These are violent and aggressive gangs that use violence as a means of getting status otherwise not available. These occur in neighborhoods that are characterized by transiency and instability, and there are no successful roles—legitimate or illegitimate—upon which a youth can model himself. The youths "seize upon the manipulation of violence as a route to status not only because it provides a way of expressing pent-up angers and frustrations, but also because they are not cut off from access to violent means by vicissitudes of birth" (Cloward and Ohlin, 1961:175). Finally, the retreatist subculture is made up of those who fail in the criminal and conflict subculture. They contend that "whether the sequence of adaptations is from criminal to retreatist or from conflict to retreatist ... limitations on legitimate and illegitimate opportunity combine to produce intense pressures toward retreatist behavior" (Cloward and Ohlin, 1961:186).

Of course, there are many other theories in which there is a strain that propels the individual toward deviancy. Those briefly discussed above serve as adequate examples, however, of why criminality is resorted to by certain individuals.

Cultural Deviance Theory

According to the theories of control and strain, individuals commit deviant acts because it is their nature or because they are pressured by external or internal strains. The cultural deviance theories, however, assume "that men are incapable of committing 'deviant' acts. A person may indeed commit acts deviant by standards of, say, middle-class society, but he cannot commit acts deviant by his own standards" (Hirschi, 1969:11). Behavior is seen to be conformity to standards that are either socially or individually determined. If the standards are society's standards, the individual is a conformist; yet, the standards reflect individual values that are not accepted by society, the behavior is labeled deviant. Theories of cultural deviance center on socialization to a socially unacceptable set of standards. Problematic are the conditions under which such learning or socialization takes place.

The first massive effort to compile statistics and do research on criminology in the United States took place at the Department of Sociology of the University of Chicago in the 1920s. This group of researchers has come to be known as the "Chicago School." These researchers looked at the particular life styles or cultures of parts of cities, groups of people, and geographic areas. Their overall conclusion was "that human beings group themselves by categories of learned influences" (Nettler, 1974:119).

The most extensive of the studies, *Juvenile Delinquency*

and Urban Areas, was published in 1942. This, and subsequent editions, pointed to the fact that more crime takes place in certain areas than in others. The *concentric circle theory* proposes that the highest rate of delinquency is found in the central business district of a city or that area zoned for industry and commerce (Shaw and McKay, 1969:55). The least amount of delinquency was found to occur in the residential areas away from the center of the city. Shaw and McKay established five two-mile-wide zones or concentric circles emanating from the center of the city (1969:67). The highest rate of delinquency occurred in the first circle and the rate decreased as the distance from the center of the city increased (Shaw and McKay, 1969:106). Yet, the data alone means nothing until the probable causes for the predominance of delinquency are considered. Fox states (1976:80), "This concentration of delinquents and criminals tends to be in areas of physical deterioration, congested population, economic dependency, rented homes, foreign and negro populations, and few institutions supported by residents. These are places in which there are few antidelinquency influences." It is indeed likely and highly probable that individuals exposed to such a deprived environment would develop their own standards of conduct that would not coincide with social standards.

In the same frame of reference and at the same time, another Chicagoan, Fredric Thrasher, studied over 1000 gangs in Chicago (1927). He maintained that gangs were the result of the social disorganization characteristic of the inner city and slums. William Whyte later disputed this theory and brought the inner-city gang, as well as the inner-city studies, into the realm of cultural deviance theories. He maintained (Whyte, 1943) that slums and inner-city areas *are* socially organized areas but that the inhabitants are often socialized to a set of standards that conflict with the standards of society.

An extension of this rationale was the basis of a classic study by Walter Miller (1958). His is perhaps the best example of cultural deviance theories. He maintained that working-class values actually include delinquency values; thus the culture *generates* delinquent subcultures. It is the concern for toughness and manliness within the working class, and the socialization to working-class values which form the impetus for subcultures that the majority of society view as deviant.

One other type of cultural deviance theory remains to be discussed. The *culture conflict theory* proposed by Thorsten Sellin (1938) holds that "crime must be analyzed in terms of conflict among *norms*" (Reid, 1974:194). He contends that for each individual there is a right and a wrong way of acting and that the definitions of right and wrong are governed by the groups to which the individual belongs. If the norms of the individual conflict with the norms of society, Sellin terms it "culture conflict." These conflicts "grow out of the process of social differentiation which characterizes the evolution of our own culture" (Sellin, 1938:105). Societal growth that increases the number of social groups also increases cultural conflicts.

Cultural deviance theories indicate that deviance is "behavior frowned upon by outsiders and not by insiders" (Hirschi, 1969:11), and a person becomes criminal by being socialized to values that happen to be different from the majority's values. This same belief with some additional qualifications forms the bases of several symbolic interactionist theories.

Symbolic Interactionist Theories

Symbolic interactionism forms the basis of many criminological theories. Actually, its influence could easily be indicated in the cultural deviance theories presented in the preceding section. The two principal types of theories that will be presented here, *differential association* and *labeling,* are perhaps the most influential theories in criminology.

Symbolic interactionism is a way of looking at the world.

It views society as being ordered to the extent that its individuals are developed or socialized. For group life to be possible there must be interaction between group members, and actions are in response to or in relation to one another. The explanations of social behavior are found in individuals' "learned dispositions identified through their expression in symbols. These dispositions are variously called 'attitudes,' 'beliefs,' 'meanings,' 'perceptions,' 'expectations,' 'values,' and 'definitions of the situation' " (Nettler, 1974:193).

According to Blumer, who coined the term *symbolic interactionism* in 1937, the perspective contains three premises (1969:2): "The first premise is that human beings act toward things on the basis of the meanings that the things have for them." If a person encounters an object that has a hostile meaning as far as he is concerned, regardless of the validity of that conception, he will act or react to the object on the basis of that meaning. "The second premise is that the meaning of such things is derived from, or arises out of, the social interaction that one has with one's fellows." Additionally, if someone interacts with certain people more often than with others, and if those with whom he interacts are "significant others" or those individuals who are held in high esteem by the person, the influence of those "differential interactions" will be greater than other associations. The third premise is that these meanings are handled in, and modified through, an interpretative process used by the person in dealing with the things he encounters.

Cultural deviance theories emphasize the culture or the social organization, yet for symbolic interactionism "social organization is a framework inside of which acting units develop their actions. Structural features, such as 'culture,' 'social systems,' 'social stratification,' or 'social roles' set conditions for action but do not determine action. People—that is, acting units—do not act toward culture, social structure, or the like; they act toward situations" (Blumer, 1969:87–88).

Differential association was first proposed as an explanation of criminal behavior by Edwin H. Sutherland in 1939. The theory is based on the laws of learning and includes the concepts of symbolic interactionism. The final theory of differential association includes the following propositions (Sutherland and Cressey, 1978:80–82):

1. Criminal behavior is learned.
2. Criminal behavior is learned in interaction with other persons in a process of communication.
3. The principal part of the learning of criminal behavior occurs within intimate personal groups.
4. When criminal behavior is learned, the learning includes: (a) techniques of committing the crime, which are sometimes very complicated, sometimes very simple; (b) the specific direction of motives, drives, rationalizations, and attitudes.
5. The specific direction of motives and drives is learned from definitions of the legal codes as favorable or unfavorable.
6. A person becomes delinquent because of an excess of definitions favorable to violation of law over definitions unfavorable to violation of law.
7. Differential associations may vary in frequency, duration, priority, and intensity.
8. The process of learning criminal behavior is by association with criminal and anti-criminal patterns.

In the first elements of his propositions, Sutherland is saying that a person becomes a criminal in the same way that he becomes anything else, including a law-abiding person—through the "learning" of behavior. This learning takes place through interaction with others. In terms of symbolic interactionism, we could say that the meaning of the law as an object arises out of one's interaction or association with others. The "intimate personal groups," implying significant others, form the models for the learning. The law, or more appropriately, socially accepted behavior, as an object is seen to be favorable or unfavorable, depending on the influence of one's associates.

Sutherland's theory points to social factors as being neither innately good nor innately bad, but simply present to be acted upon by others. The social organization is defined by those actions that take place within it. This contention differentiates symbolic interactionist theories from the cultural deviance theories.

The essential idea is that criminal behavior is learned through interaction with people. The specific direction of motives, drives, rationalizations, and attitudes toward criminality or anti-criminality is learned from individuals or groups who define the law as something to be observed, or from those whose definitions favor the violation of the law. These two kinds of definitions exist side by side in today's society, and a person receives contradictory definitions from others. Sutherland calls this process of receiving two kinds of definitions *differential association* because what is learned in association with criminal behavior patterns is in competition with what is learned in association with anti-criminal behavior patterns. When a person becomes a criminal he does so because of an excessive exposure to criminal behavior patterns and an isolation from anti-criminal behavior patterns.

The adequacy of differential association theory has been criticized on a number of positions. Caldwell (1956:181-185) pointed out a number of weaknesses of the theory. Nettler (1974:196-199) discussed the inadequacies and neglected areas of the theory. Adams (1974:1-8) stated that differential association "cannot be expected to adequately explain or predict criminal behavior." Yet, others say that the theory "is probably the most powerful theory in the field of criminology—that is to say, it makes sense of the greatest range of facts about crime" (Cohen and Short, 1971:126). It is not within the purview of this discussion to debate the merits or demerits of Sutherland's theory, but simply to briefly explain the major points of the theory to show its contribution to the evolution of criminology.

A perspective that has recently gained tremendous prominence in criminology is *labeling theory*. This theory has taken a stronghold in criminological thought, although the perspective itself is not new. Frank Tannenbaum wrote in the late 1930s (1938:20):

The person becomes the thing he is described as being. [It does not] seem to matter whether the valuation is made by those who would punish or by those who would reform. The parents or the policeman, the older brother or the court, the probation officer or the juvenile institution, in so far as they rest upon the thing complained of, rest upon a false ground. Their very enthusiasm defeats their aim. The harder they work to reform the evil, the greater the evil grows under their hands.

In another section, Tannenbaum states this idea more succinctly (1938:19-20): "The process of making the criminal ... is a process of tagging, defining, identifying, segregating, describing, emphasizing, making conscious and self-conscious; it becomes a way of stimulating, suggesting, emphasizing, and evoking the very traits complained of. ... The person becomes the thing he is described as being." Tannenbaum, and after him Lemert, Becker, Schur, and a host of others, redirected the attention from the actor or criminal to the system or process of becoming criminal. The labeling perspective emphasizes the *process* and does not see deviance as a state entity but as an outcome of social interaction. It has been characterized as a "theory of deviant roles rather than a theory of the deviant act" (Hawkins and Tiedman, 1975:43). This shift in emphasis was begun in differential association and personified in labeling.

The labeling perspective owes many of its propositions to symbolic interactionism. W. I. Thomas, one of the founders of symbolic interactionism, stated, "if men define situations as real, they are real in their consequences" (1928:572). George Herbert Mead (1934) viewed the "self" as a social object; therefore, behavior of the self is an ever-emerging product. Blumer (1969) also emphasized the self as a social object which was formed and transformed by interaction with others.

Schrag identified what is considered the basic assumptions of labeling theory (1971:89-91):

1. No act is intrinsically criminal.
2. Criminal definitions are enforced in the interest of the powerful.
3. A person does not become a criminal by violation of the law but

only by the designation of criminality by authorities.
4. Due to the fact that everyone conforms and deviates, people should not be dichotomized into criminal and noncriminal categories.
5. The act of "getting caught" begins the labeling process.
6. "Getting caught" and the decision making in the criminal justice system are a function of the offender as opposed to offense characteristics.
7. Age, socio-economic class, and race are the major offender characteristics that establish patterns of differential criminal justice decision making.
8. The criminal justice system is established on a free-will perspective that allows for the condemnation and rejection of the identified offender.
9. Labeling is a process that produces, eventually, identification with a deviant image and subculture, and a resulting "rejection of the rejectors."

Though Schrag characterizes each of these as an "assumption," it has been suggested that most˙ of the elements should be considered hypotheses (Wellford, 1975:332).

The labeling perspective can best be viewed as a dialectic involving the actor and the audience (Davis, 1975:182), in which the actor is stigmatized as "different." Once typed or labeled, the acts are interpreted in accordance with the status.

An important concept within labeling was discussed by Lemert (1951:76–77). He did not feel that one incident and the reaction to that incident was enough to cause the person to then become the thing he was described as being. He contended that there would be a series of actions, reactions, and counteractions before the actor identified with the criminal image. In the first action or series of actions, denials, neutralizations, or other attempts to normalize the offenses might be used. The causes of the actions or "primary deviation" might be strain, lack of socialization, socialization to deviant values, or differential association. However, once the accused "begins to employ his deviant behavior, or a role based on it, as a means of defense, attack, or adjustment to the overt and covert problems created by the consequent societal reaction to him, his deviation is secondary" (Lemert, 1951:76).

3. The New Criminology: A Review of the Literature

The purpose for presenting a detailed account of early criminological theories as they evolved from the Classical School through to the various positivistic perspectives was to show the shifts in emphasis and focal points in the study of criminality. In the beginning of the examination of these theories, it was obvious that the act and not the actor was the point of consideration. As scientific technology progressed, the focus of enquiry became the actor. In the latter stages of attempts to explain criminality, however, the focus seems to have shifted to the society in general and the criminal justice system in specific. The evolution of criminology has set the stage for the "New Criminology" which incorporates many of the concepts of the labeling perspective and shifts the blame from actor to society itself.

Before discussing the New Criminology and the variety of perspectives subsumed by that term, the discipline of criminal justice will be discussed. Criminal justice is obviously an integral consideration in any study of crime and criminality because it is the task of that institution to maintain order and enforce the law.

Criminal Justice

Criminology, as a discipline, is concerned with the development of a body of knowledge regarding the making of laws, the breaking of laws, and society's reaction to the breaking of laws. "Criminal justice is mostly concerned with the decision process in the crime control agencies of police, prosecutors' offices, trial courts, and correctional facilities, and in programs like probation and parole" (Newman, 1978:5). The criminal justice system, then, is the system responsible for reacting, in the name of society, to the breaking of laws. Criminal justice is both a *discipline* and a *system*.

The academic discipline of criminal justice can be traced to the early part of the twentieth century when August Vollmer taught the first crime-related courses at the University of California at Berkeley. In 1929 the University of Chicago also created a police training program as a part of the curriculum in the department of political science. Some of the courses offered by these programs were Police Administration and Police Procedure.

Various institutions initiated police science or criminal justice courses at a steady pace up to 1965. These programs were modeled after the Berkeley and Michigan State University programs, both founded by August Vollmer, and the emphasis was on training individuals to administer the criminal justice system. The criminal justice discipline experienced a phenomenal growth rate in the late 1960s and early 1970s. By 1973 the number of institutions offering criminal justice programs, as reflected by the institutions participating in the Law Enforcement Education Program, had reached almost 700. Unfortunately, the rampant growth in criminal justice education programs has caused some to question the credibility of the discipline due to the lack of a well-founded theoretical base.

The discipline of criminal justice is viewed by some as being totally separate from the study of criminology. Others view the former as being an integral aspect of the latter. Criminal justice is seen by some as *applied criminology*, and for others it is an area for academic concern on the part of criminologists. Whether the two areas—criminal justice and criminology—are seen as one discipline or two mutually exclusive disciplines, none can rebut the fact that the two are closely intertwined.

The main difference in the two approaches seems to be the usage of and emphasis upon the law. Criminology views the law as that which designates the area of study—criminal behavior. "Criminal behavior is behavior in violation of a criminal law. No matter what the degree of immorality, reprehensibility, or indecency of an act, it is not a criminal act unless it is outlawed by the state" (Sutherland and Cressey, 1978:4). Criminal justice, on the other hand, is a "legal entity." "All the agencies, offices, and programs in criminal justice exist by law and are controlled by the legal process" (Newman, 1977:5). Where criminology uses the law as a tool to define its area of interest, criminal justice is formed and defined by the criminal law.

The emphasis in criminal justice is on the legal definition of crime. This reflects or compliments the perspective of the Classical School: "The doctrine of the Classical School is *nullen crimen sine lege,* that is, without a legally defined harm there is no crime" (Jeffery, 1956:664). The focus of concern is upon the act and who committed it. Perhaps the fact that criminal justice is classical and criminology is positivistic accounts for the lack of continuity, and sometimes open animosity, between the two perspectives.

Perspectives Within the New Criminology

While tracing the development of criminology in the previous chapter, certain trends became obvious. Each theory gained prominence at the point where the previous perspective was closest to it in terms of domain and assumptions. The new perspective would grow in prominence, acceptance, and empirical testing that would result in variations of the perspective—variations that would eventually lead to another paradigm.

Certainly at this point in the study of criminological thought, all of the positions and perspectives subsumed by the New Criminology must be delineated. As was said by Goethe and quoted in the epigraph of Louis Coser's book

(1971), "What you have inherited from your fathers, acquire it in order to possess it," has particular meaning for the study of the New Criminology. Contemporary positions within the paradigm can only be understood in light of the contributions of those who constructed the foundation for the present position.

The term "the *New Criminology*" is as yet a temporary one. An indication of this was the composition of a panel on "new criminology" at the 1978 annual conference of the Academy of Criminal Justice Sciences. The panel was made up of proponents of *conflict-critical-radical-Marxian criminology* and *psycho-biological criminology*. Certainly these were vastly different perspectives; yet both were under the umbrella of the New Criminology. The purpose of this chapter is to closely define what is meant by the "new criminology" by tracing the development and outlining the major points of view within the perspective.

Conflict Theory as a Basis of the New Criminology

The new criminology reflected by conflict-critical-radical-Marxian theories of deviance formed as an extension of the conflict theory in sociology. As theories of deviance, each perspective has taken on diverse titles, sometimes more like crusading issues than descriptive titles, and each of these theories will be studied. First, it is necessary to develop the foundation for all of the new theories in criminology by carefully studying the conflict paradigm in sociology.

The ideology and rationale of Karl Marx has played a very important part in contemporary sociology. One prominent criminologist stated: "A major structural characteristic of Western Sociology develops after the emergence of Marxism: Following this, Western Sociology is divided into two camps, each with its own continuums, intellectual tradition, and distinctive intellectual paradigms, and each greatly insulated from or mutually contemptuous of the other" (Gouldner, 1970:111). The reason for this condition is the Marxists' "expressions of the existence of an unfilled theoretical need that derives from the gap between their own new structure of sentiments or their own sense of what is real, on the one hand, and, on the other hand, the older theories now available in the academic and social surround" (Gouldner, 1970:7). Given the obvious importance of Marxian theory to sociology and its influence later on theories of deviance, it is beneficial to engage in a brief discussion of the major points of Marxian theory.

Marx viewed man as "a perpetually dissatisfied animal" (Coser, 1971:43). It is man's nature to struggle against nature in order to gratify his needs; yet when the needs have been met, man creates new needs. For Marx, "struggle rather than peaceful growth was the engine of progress; strife was the father of all things, and social conflict the core of historical process" (Coser, 1971:43). The wresting of man's livelihood from nature was seen as the motivating force in history. The history of all society, then, "is the history of class struggles" (Marx 1888 in Truzzi, 1971:204):

> The division of labor offers us the first example of how, as long as man remains in natural society (governed by laws which are inexorable, like natural laws over which men have no control) that is as long as a cleavage exists between the particular and the common interests, as long therefore as activity is not voluntary, but naturally, divided, man's own deed becomes an alien power opposed to him, which enslaves him instead of being controlled by him. For as soon as labor is distributed, each man has a particular, exclusive sphere of activity, which is forced upon him and from which he cannot escape (Marx and Engels, 1960:22).

Marx maintained that "the sum total of the relations of production, that is, the relations men establish with each other when they utilize existing raw materials and technologies in the pursuit of their productive goals constitute the real foundations upon which the whole cultural superstructure of society comes to be erected" (Coser, 1971:45). All relations—social and technical—are entered into by and for the participation in economic life. "The mode of production of material life determines the general character of the social, political, and spiritual processes of life. It is not the consciousness of men that determines their being, but, on the contrary, their social being determines their consciousness" (Marx, 1964:51). This dehumanization of man was viewed as a result of alienation according to one writer (Zeitun, 1968:86). Marx uses the term "alienation" in two ways. The first, *entäussern,* means "to part with," "to give up," "to divest one's self of." This term relates directly to property. The other term that is translated to mean alienation is *enfremden,* which means two people becoming estranged from one another. In a capitalistic society, men are forced to part with the materials produced unless they control the means of production. "The object produced by labor, its product, now stands opposed to [its producers] as an alien being, as a power independent of the producer. ... The more the worker expends himself in work the more powerful becomes the world of objects which he creates in face of himself, the poorer he becomes in his inner life, and the less he becomes to himself" (Marx, 1964:122). Therefore, alienation, as a result of one class owning the means of production and another class involved in production, causes a person to be separated from the object he produces and from himself. "In work he does not belong to himself but to another person" (Marx, 1964:125). Marx further contended (1964:129) "Man is alienated from other men. When man confronts himself he also confronts other men. What is true of man's relationship to his work, to the product of his work, and to himself, is also true of his relationship to other men. ... Each man is alienated from others. ... Each of the others is likewise alienated from human life."

The cause of alienation, and a subsequent economic substructure, is the class system. Marx analyzed the class system as to how relationships, including alienation, between men are shaped by their relative positions in regard to the means of production. Unequal access to the means of production, synonymous with power, provides the potential for class conflict. Quinney states (1977:64-65), "class analysis ... begins with the fundamental dynamic of capitalism: the dialectic between two opposing forces—preservation of the existing relationships and modification or destruction of these relationships. Class is thus the necessary concept in a Marxist analysis of the inner workings of capitalist society." The Marxian model of capitalistic society involves two classes, a *superordinate* class—the *bourgeoisie,* and a *subordinate* class—the *proletariat.* In each class, there is a common interest for or against the status quo. Over a period of time, Marx contended, the proletariat inevitably develops an awareness of bourgeoisie concerns—self-interest and exploitation. This awareness or class consciousness leads to greater conflict and separation between the two classes.

An excellent synopsis of the major propositions of Marx's conflict theory is presented by Turner (1974:82):

I. The more unequal the distribution of scarce resources in a system, the more conflict of interest between dominant and subordinate segments in a system.

II. The more subordinate segments become aware of their true collective interests, the more likely they are to question the legitimacy of the existing pattern of distribution of scarce resources.
   A. The more social changes wrought by dominant segments disrupt existing relations among subordinates, the more likely the subordinates become aware of their true interests.
   B. The more practices of dominant segments create alienation ... among subordinates, the more likely are the subordinates to become aware of their true collective interests.
   C. The more members of subordinate segments can communicate their grievances to each other, the more likely they are to become aware of their true collective interests.
      1. The more ecological concentration of members of subordinate groups, the more likely communication of grievances [will take place.]
      2. The more the educational opportunities of subordinate group members, the more diverse the means of their communication, and the more likely they are to communicate their grievances.
   D. The more subordinate segments can develop unifying ideologies, the more likely they are to become aware of their true collective interest.

1. The greater the capacity to recruit or generate ideological spokesmen, the more likely ideological unification [will take place].
2. The less the ability of dominant groups to regulate the socialization processes and communication networks in a system, the more likely ideological unification [will take place].

III. The more subordinate segments of a system are aware of their collective interest and the greater their questioning of the legitimacy of the distribution of scarce resources, the more likely they are to join overt conflict against dominant segments of a system.
   A. The less ability dominant groups have to make manifest their collective interests, the more likely subordinate groups are to join in conflict.
   B. The more deprivations of subordinates move from an absolute to relative basis, the more likely they are to join in conflict.
   C. The greater the ability of subordinate groups to develop a political leadership structure, the more likely they are to join in conflict.
IV. The greater the ideological unification of members of subordinate segments of a system and the more developed their political leadership structure, the more polarized the dominant and subjugated segments of a system.
V. The more polarized the dominant and subjugated, the more violent the conflict will be.
VI. The more violent the conflict, the more structural change of the system and the greater the redistribution of scarce resources.

In sum, Marx began with the assumption that the economic organization determines the organization of the rest of society. Unless the society is a pure communistic society, conflict over the economic organization is inevitable. This conflict will escalate and bipolarize society. The conflict will ultimately result in social change. At that point, when the bourgeoisie economic organization has been overthrown, "the prehistory of human society will have come to an end" and harmony will replace conflict (Marx, 1964:52–53). Though Marx did not speak directly to the issue of crime and criminality, his theory of social organization has supplied the terms and concepts for the conflict perspective in criminology.

Ralf Dahrendorf has been viewed as the foremost contemporary sociologist representing the dialectical conflict perspective. Dahrendorf maintained that society has two faces—one is the consensual, integrated social model of functionalism and the other is that of change, conflict, and constraint. He does not contend that the conflict perspective is the only perspective, but that conflict and consensus have "equal reality"; yet because of past inadequacies of functionalism, conflict predominates.

A most important concept contained in the work of Dahrendorf was the idea of basic units of social organization or *imperatively coordinated associates* (1959:171). In earlier writings he labeled these units "imperatively co-ordinated groups" (1958b); yet the use of "associates" seems to translate more adequately the unity Dahrendorf intended. "There is a large number of imperatively co-ordinated associations in any given society. Within every one of them we can distinguish the aggregates of those who dominate and those who are subjected" (Dahrendorf, 1959:171). The important point in Dahrendorf's argument is that he substituted the concept of authority for that of class and rejected the centrality of class as the source of conflict.

Power and authority are the resources that are competed for among social units. They are, according to Dahrendorf, the sources of class conflict. And this conflict ultimately leads to social change. The differences in Dahrendorf's ideas and those of Marx are illustrated in the following quotation:

> For Marx, the source of conflict ultimately lay beneath cultural values and institutional arrangements which represented edifices constructed by those with power. In reality, the dynamics of society are found in society's 'subculture,' where the differential distribution of property and power inevitably initiates a sequence of events leading, under specifiable conditions, to revolutionary class conflict. . . . Dahrendorf actually ends up positing a much different source of conflict: the institutionalized authority relations of [imperatively co-ordinated associations]. Such a position is much different from that

of Marx, who viewed such authority relations as simply a 'superstructure' erected by the dominant classes, which, in the long run, would be destroyed by the conflict dynamics occurring below institutional arrangements. While Dahrendorf acknowledges that authority relations are imposed by the dominant groups in [imperatively co-ordinated associations], ... [t]he source of conflict becomes, upon closer examination, the legitimated authority role relations of the [imperatively co-ordinated associations]. (Turner, 1974:95)

Dahrendorf's drift from the Marxian view of the class-cause of conflict in the social organization has led some to label him a proponent of *conflict-functionalism* (Taylor, et. al., 1973:266). Still the arguments of these two—Marx and Dahrendorf—form the basis for the views of the new conflict theorists who concern themselves with crime and criminology.

Conflict Criminology

George Vold wrote the first criminological textbook (1958) which was almost exclusively devoted to explaining crime and criminality from a social conflict point of view. Vold viewed society as being involved in social conflict which "is said to be a universal form of interaction" (Vold, 1958:203). His theory tends to be non-Marxian. In fact, he views Marx's only contribution to criminology to be in the area of economic determinism (Vold, 1958:160). Vold's description of society is detailed in the first portion of his chapter entitled "Group Conflict Theory of Crime" (1958:204-205):

> As social interaction processes grind their way through varying kinds of uneasy adjustments to a more or less stable equilibrium of balanced forces in opposition, the resulting condition of relative stability is what is usually called social order or social organization. But it is the adjustment, one to another, of the many groups of varying strengths and of different interests that is the essence of society as functioning reality.

The "groups" Vold refers to are very similar to Dahrendorf's "imperatively co-ordinated associations," but Vold provides an analysis of the *raison d'etre* of the groups. "Groups are forced out of situations in which members have common interests and common needs that can best be furthered through collective action." However, if the groups do not serve the interests and needs of the members, they eventually dissolve (Vold, 1958:205).

In Vold's concept of society there seems to be the orderly growth of social units. Conflict occurs between the groups "as the interests and purposes they serve tend to overlap, encroach on one another and be competitive" (Vold, 1958:205). The conflict between groups is primarily one of survival. The competition is over common needs and interests, so the group that gains these scarce commodities is capable of replacing the other group. "The principal goal, therefore, of one group in contact with another, is to keep from being replaced" (Vold, 1958:205).

The functional aspects of group conflict include loyalty and identification with the group. "It has long been realized that conflict between groups tends to develop and intensify the loyalty of group members to their respective groups" (Vold, 1958:206). Group cohesiveness or *esprit de corps* promotes harmony and self-sacrifice.

The result of social conflict is "conquest and victory for one side with the utter defeat and destruction or subjugation from the other side. ... The weak, as a rule, are quickly overwhelmed, subjugated to and integrated with victors in some subordinate and inferior capacity" (Vold, 1958:207). A means of establishing and maintaining the subjugation of the weak to the dominant in society is the enactment of laws and control of the enforcement of those laws. These laws, specifically the criminal laws, favor the conquerors at the expense, in terms of criminality, of the conquered. "The whole political process of law making, law breaking, and law enforcement becomes a direct reflection of deep-seated and fundamental conflicts between interest groups..." (Vold, 1958:208–209). This is a direct reference to Sutherland's sociological definition of the study of crime which Vold neatly positions in the group conflict theory of crime. Vold further argues that another major result of conflict is the control of the police power in society. "Those who produce legislative majorities win control over the police power and dominate the policies that decide who is likely to be involved in violation of the law" (Vold, 1958:209). Therefore, conflict results in the conquered or minority being classified as criminals more often than the majority or powerful. Within this framework, Vold implies that crime, according to Sutherland's definition, would be acceptable as a social situation rather than "as an act of behavior under specific legal definition" (1958:209).

Vold's ideological stance on a number of issues is evident by his treatment of the various theories of criminality. "The first and foremost condition that needs to be recognized is the basic dichotomy inherent in all explanations given for the events with which man is involved" (1958:305). This dichotomy is demonism or *spiritualism* versus *naturalism*. This could be restated as "other world" powers versus "this world" influences. Though he recognized the "other world" powers—"spiritualism is a matter of faith"—he considered only naturalistic theories in the discussion of the causes of crime because this approach was more systematic and scientific.

Vold identified three general types of naturalistic theories (1958:306): (1) those that emphasize the individual, (2) those that emphasize group and inter-group relations, and (3) those that are "eclectical" and include all factors that might be of importance. The theories that emphasize the individual are most often related to positivism. They can be viewed from the physiological or biological point of concentration, the psychological or psychiatric orientation or, from the point of view of what Vold terms, *individualistic eclectic theories,* which consider several elements from different orientations, all focusing on the individual and his deficiencies or disturbances. The group behavior theories, Vold contends, can be placed in two categories. One is the normal learning approach and the belief that crime is normal and accepted behavior considering the group to which the individual belongs. The other category of group theories, and certainly the one which Vold espouses, "rationalizes [crime] in terms of conflict. ... Crime is considered to be the expression of individual behavior in the situation in which groups are in conflict with one another" (1958:309). All individuals in society are viewed as soldiers for various sides with various interests, and all are dedicated to winning the battle for power:

> The individual criminal is then viewed as essentially a soldier under conditions of warfare: his behavior may not be 'normal' or 'happy' or 'adjusted'—it is the behavior of the soldier doing what is to be done in wartime. The analogy is with group conflict and warfare, not with the mental hospital or the individualistic approach of the psychiatric lunatic (Vold, 1958:309).

The last category of naturalistic theories Vold labels *general eclecticism*. This theory rejects the possibility of any one explanation of criminality. Extreme eclecticism Vold views as "the equivalant of no theory at all" (1958:310). He discusses these types of theories as "tending to reject and deny the possibility of making valid generalizations out of the assorted information at hand" (1958:310).

It would be a mistake to classify Vold as a positivist since he rejects the individualist theories of criminality and accepts the conflict theory. He states in his "Preface" (1958:vii):

> No special plea is made for any particular theoretical position examined, though it should be clear that there is some preference for approaches that recognize and make more explicit the concept of crime as a by-product of the struggle for power in the group structure of society.

With this orientation, Vold does not locate the causes of crime in anything prior to the group conflict, but views social conflict as the ultimate cause of crime. He also seems to accept the consensual view of the law. "Those who reject the *majority* view and refuse to follow required behavior patterns are inevitably defined as, and treated as, criminals" (1958:213).

Vold's view of crime and criminality corresponds closely with the views held by those proponents of symbolic interactionism. Crime and criminality are *definitions* of certain behavior and actions. The importance of Vold's contribution is that it placed a new area of consideration in the criminological spectrum—*conflict criminology*. As is true of the first of a series of theories, Vold's is not as well defined or as soundly based as those which followed.

Austin Turk is one of the most eloquent and steadfast of all of the contemporary conflict theorists. He seems to follow Dahrendorf's framework for a sociological conflict theory and further develops his own explanation of deviance. Turk's concern is with an explanation of criminality as reflected by his first major work, *Criminality and Legal Order* (1969). The major contention of the book is that "under certain social conditions some individuals are more likely than others to be criminalized" (Keller, 1976:102). He views criminality as a status, and it is this aspect that should be examined rather than criminal etiology. "Nothing and no one is intrinsically criminal; criminality is a definition applied by individuals with the power to do so, according to illegal and extra-legal, as well as legal criteria" (Turk, 1969:10). Though this sounds much like the labeling perspective discussed earlier, Turk goes beyond its propositions. He agrees that law breaking cannot be distinguished from conformity except by the label or status of criminality, but he also explains the milieu that establishes the social categories (1969:18):

> Unless one assumes that legal processes somehow operate in a vacuum, entirely apart from the conflicts intrinsic to social relations—an assumption now rather thoroughly discredited—it is unreasonable to suppose that differences in criminality rates among different categories of people are solely due to corresponding variations in their behavior patterns. Therefore, instead of assuming the criminality of some of the behavior patterns of persons in certain social categories, and proceeding to look for the sources of the behavior patterns presumably to explain their criminality (a neat circle), one is led to investigate the tendency of laws to penalize persons whose behavior is more characteristic of the less powerful than of the more powerful

and the extent to which some persons and groups can and do use legal processes and agencies to maintain and enhance their power position *vis-a-vis* other persons and groups.

Turk maintains that the situation society finds itself in is one of conflict between groups seeking to gain or maintain control over the others (1969:30–52). The law is the instrument of control. If the control is effective and the subjects accept their position, laws are not violated. If, however, the authorities and subjects are in conflict, the law is imposed as a means of coercion—"law breaking is a measure of the extent to which ruler and ruled, decision makers and decision acceptors, are not bound together in a perfectly stable relationship" (1969:48).

In *Criminality and Legal Order* (1969), Turk rejects behavioral explanations of "causes" of criminality. Just as Vold before him, Turk states that "it is more useful to view the social order as mainly a pattern of conflict" and not of consensus (1969:50). In order to understand criminality, the social scientist must understand the "basically coercive relationship of communities" (1969:50).

Turk constructs a general theory of criminalization that specifies the conditions which lead to an authority-subject relationship labeled *authority-criminal.* Some of the key propositions of Turk's theory indicate his indebtedness to the labeling perspective and to Dahrendorf's view of authority. He introduces his theory as one with an *interactionist* framework (1969:53):

> A sociological theory of interaction is required; moreover, it must be a theory of interaction among groupings and categories of people rather than a social psychological explanation of patterns in interaction among individuals, even though psychological assumptions will necessarily be implicit in any such theory.

Turk's acceptance of at least some of the propositions of the labeling theory is evident in his key statements. He says, for instance, that the criminality rate "is that proportion of a social category which has been defined as 'criminal' by the actions of legal norm enforcers" (1969:105). He is implying that the criminality rate is not strictly official statistics but includes those which have been classified, identified, or defined as "norm resisters" and will likely receive the label of criminal (1969:106). Earlier in his book Turk gives his explanation or definition of "criminal"—"anyone who is defined officially as a violator ... is criminal in the general sense (1969:13). Elsewhere, Turk comes closer to the labeling assumptions by stating (1969:18), "if predilections are to be avoided, a criminal is most accurately defined as any individual who is identified as such."

Labeling theorists see criminality as a label; Turk sees criminality as a status. There seems to be no difference in the two views except the manner in which the label-status is applied. Turk states (1969:64):

> Generally we expect that the greater the behavioral significance of the legal norm for authorities, both in regard to congruence of cultural and social norms, and in regard to the relative priority of the norm over other norms, the greater the probability that violators will be assigned criminal status.

In an earlier work (1966:334), Turk further explains the way in which the label is applied: "a person is evaluated, either favorably or unfavorably, not because he does something, or even because he is something, but because others react to their perceptions of him as offensive or inoffensive."

Turk subscribes to the Dahrendorf style of conflict as opposed to the Marxian theory. This is obvious in his substitution of the Weberian concept of authority for the Marxian concept of class in determining the central source of conflict in society. Turk states (1969:35):

> The study of criminality becomes the study of relations between statuses and roles of legal authorities—creators, interpreters, and enforcers or right-wrong standards for individuals in the political collectivity—and those of subjects—acceptors or resisters but not makers of such law creating, interpreting, and enforcing decisions.

In a recent work (1977), Turk delineates the basic differences and similarities between the Marxian and Weberian views as to the meanings of class, conflict, and criminality.

Though he compliments labeling theory as having "contributed to greater sensitivity among researchers to the distinctions between observed and reported or imputed acts, between exploratory and career behavior, between behavioral and nonbehavioral criteria of deviance, and between reactive and proactive modes of social control," Turk maintains that labeling has generally ignored the social structure as an integral element of consideration. By the same token, he maintains that Merton's "analysis of the relationship between class structure and deviance rates" has provided a valuable tool to social scientists while ignoring obvious inequalities (1977:209). Turk further contends that the "new criminologists," using anomie and labeling ideas, can be dichotomized as those opting for Marxian theory and those inclined toward the Weberian theory of authority.

Both Marxian and Weberian theorists agree that "laws, law breaking, and law enforcement originate in and contribute to patterns of social conflict and disproportionate power" while rejecting biological, psychological, or functionalistic explanations of legality and illegality (1977:210). The Marxian perspective views class differences as the source of conflict. "Class differences in both the behavior and the labeling of crime are attributed to class differences in opportunities and power within a legal system designed to facilitate rather than stop the exploitation of workers by the bourgeoisie" (Turk, 1977:215). The sources of conflict for the Weberian theorist are the cultural and social structures. Classes are merely social categories. "The conflicts that generate law making and breaking are attributed to the efforts of various kinds of interest groups to attain and use power for their own protection (Turk, 1977:215).

In a paper published in an issue of *Criminology,* Turk delineates the working premises for his theory of deviance (Turk, 1978:9-10):

1. Individuals diverge in their understandings and commitments.
2. Divergence leads, under specifiable conditions, to conflict.

3. Each conflicting party tries to promote its own understandings and commitments.
4. The result is a more or less conscious struggle over the distribution of available resources, and therefore, of life changes.
5. People with similar understandings and commitments tend to join forces, and people who stay together tend to develop similar understandings and commitments.
6. Continuing conflicts tend to become routinized in the form of stratification systems.
7. Such systems (at least at the intergroup level) are characterized by economic exploitation sustained by political domination in all forms from most clearly violent to the most subtly ideological.
8. The relative power of conflicting parties determines their hierarchical position; changes in position reflect only changes in the distribution of power.
9. Convergence in understandings and commitments is generated by the (not necessarily voluntary) sharing of experiences in dealing with "insiders," "outsiders," and the neutral environment.
10. The relationship between divergence and convergence in human understandings and commitments is a dialectical one; ergo, the basic social process of dynamics is one of conflict.

Turk's contribution to the sociology of deviance in general and conflict criminology specifically has been significant. His is a more conservative or traditional form of conflict theory than some propose, which is possibly why he is criticized in some criminological circles. Some critics (Marzotto et al., 1975:43) have stated that Turk is ignorant of "the international nature of the modern political economy." Perhaps these criticisms can be explained by a phrase from Turk's latest paper (1978:11): "Merely being *different* becomes *deviant* insofar as the difference is one that elicits the sense of threat, in ways from the most subtle to the most obvious."

In William Chambliss' and Robert Seidman's *Law, Order and Power* (1971), they began their analysis by presenting two models of society. These "two very general models of society purport to answer the question whether society is based on a value-consensus or a value-antagonism" (Chambliss and Seidman, 1971:17). The arrangement presented is very similar to that of functionalism versus conflict which has been previously discussed. In conclusion of their discussion they maintain that the true model of society is the conflict model. Their view differs from Turk's in that theirs is certainly a Marxian view:

> In the Marxian view ... the state consists of the institutions of coercion: the police, the army, prison officials. These are the principal weapons in the hands of the ruling classes. Law, which rests finally upon the state's self-perpetuating monopoly of violence or instruments of coercion, therefore, represents the will of the ruling classes; in more modern terms, we would say that it embodies the views of the ruling class.

Chambliss and Seidman focus on social conflict and on the implication of criminal law. They attack the "central myth about the legal order ... that the normative structures of the written law represent the actual operation of the legal order" (1971:3). They do not attack the law itself but the value-loaded discretion of those who enforce, interpret, and administer the law. It is this process that they term "the legal order" which "is in fact a self-serving system to maintain power and privilege" (1971:4) rather than a vehicle to settle disputes and resolve conflict.

Each subsystem of the legal order is surveyed under the scrutiny of the conflict model. The first of the subsystems examined is the legislature. They maintain (1971:73) that "every detailed study of the emergence of legal norms has consistently shown the immense importance of interest group activity, *not* 'the *public interest*,' as the critical variable in determining the content of legislation." The powerful and the privileged are the ones with influence in legislative decision making. This ensures that they will remain the powerful and the privileged. If it were true that "what is good for General Motors is good for society," this method of special interest legislation would be acceptable; but seldom is this the case (Chambliss and Seidman, 1971:73).

Continuing in their analysis of the legal order and conflict theory, the authors examine the appellate courts. These courts are selected because if any should be value free and neutral it should be the appellate level. They examine what is termed "the principal inputs into the rule-making processes of the appellate courts" (1971:113). These inputs include issues, policies, personal attributes of judges, their socialization, situational pressures, organizational interests of the courts, and the permissible rules of law: "It is intriguing how these various inputs are necessarily biased in favor of ensuring that courts as institutions are more available to the wealthy than to the poor, and tend to produce solutions in the interests of the wealthy" (1971:113). The specific indicators include the high cost of litigation, especially at the appellate level and the recruitment and socialization of judges. All of these indicate a lack of neutrality and ensure that the "haves" keep and the "have nots" do not progress.

The institutions of the police, prosecutors, and sentencing practices are each examined and shown to be anything but value neutral. The symbolic assailant concept, discretion, negotiated pleas, and stereotypes all indicate that the system is more biased than just. The following propositions that refer to the process of law enforcement in a complex society serve as excellent examples (Chambliss and Seidman, 1971:269):

1. The agencies of law-enforcement are bureaucratic organizations.
2. An organization and its members tend to substitute for the official goals and norms of the organization's ongoing policies and activities which will maximize rewards and minimize the strains on the organization.
3. This goal substitution is made possible by:
   a. The absence of motivation on the part of the role-occupants to resist pressures toward goal-substitution.
   b. The pervasiveness of discretionary choice permitted by the substantive criminal law, and the norms defining the roles of the members of the enforcement agencies.
   c. The absence of effective sanctions for the norms defining the roles in those agencies.
4. Law enforcement agencies depend for resource allocation on political organizations.
5. It will maximize rewards and minimize strains for the organiza-

tion to process those who are politically weak and powerless, and to refrain from processing those who are politically powerful.
6. Therefore, it may be expected that the law enforcement agencies will process a disproportionately high number of the politically weak and powerless, while ignoring the violations of those with power.

It has been pointed out (Keller, 1976:129) that even though Chambliss and Seidman explicitly stated that the propositions outlined above provide a framework for understanding law enforcement, in actuality they could be seen as applicable to the entire criminal justice system. Each of the propositions describes the criminal justice system as seen through the eyes of the conflict theorists.

In stronger terminology the writers contend that organizational pressures contribute to the perpetuation of the powerful who control the decision-making process (1971:505):

> This discretion and the illegal behavior of some of those who man the bulwarks of power appear to be controlled, not by the public interest, obedience to norms, or rationality, but by naked self-interest, interest-group pressures, and irrationality.

The operation of the criminal justice system is characterized by injustice and the crusading issue revolves around what is convenient for the powerful. In this type of system "if justice or fairness happen to be served, it is sheer coincidence" (1971:503).

Perhaps the most concise view of conflict criminology, from a Marxian view, is presented by Chambliss and Seidman in the following statement (1971:504):

> ... society is composed of groups that are in conflict with one another and that the law represents an institutionalized tool of those in power (ruling class) which functions to provide them with superior moral as well as coercive power in conflict.

In a later article (1976:66–106) Chambliss indicates that he has become more radical in his views of crime and criminal law. He speaks a great deal more of the economic substructure and its influence on the bureaucracy; whereas in his earlier work (1971) he focused on the bureaucracy's impact on law and justice. His later views are within the Marxian context but much more explicit as to the causes of injustice (1976:80): "The criminal law creation process organizes into it the views of those classes who control the economic resources as a result of the entire matrix of recruitment, socialization, and situational pressures upon those who create the laws." Later, he says "the heart of a capitalist economic system is the protection of private property.... It is not surprising, then, to find that the criminal law reflects this basic concern" (1976:85). Chambliss cannot, however, fully agree with every point of the Marxian-radical contention, especially with respect to the presence of a monolithic ruling class that has freedom to do whatever it pleases, while those who are ruled sit passively, accepting the interests of the rulers (1976:101).

In his conclusion Chambliss succinctly states his key propositions concerning the study of crime and criminality (1976:101):

> Crime is a political phenomenon. What gets defined as criminal or delinquent behavior is the result of a political process within which rules are formed which prohibit or require people to behave in certain ways.... Thus to ask 'why is it that some acts get defined as criminal while others do not' is the starting point for all systematic study of crime and criminal behavior. Nothing is inherently criminal; it is only the response that makes it so.

One of the major contributions by Chambliss to the field of criminology in general and the New Criminology specifically was the formulation of his version of Conflict Criminology. The elements are taken in the original form (1975:152-153) and synthesized below:

1. Acts are defined as criminal because it is in the interests of the ruling class to so define them.
2. Members of the ruling class will be able to violate the laws with impunity while members of the subject classes will be punished.
3. As capitalistic societies industrialize, penal laws will expand in an effort to coerce the proletariat into submission.
4. Crime diverts the lower classes' attention from the exploitation

they experience and directs it toward other members of their own class rather than toward the capitalist class or the economic system.
5. Crime is a reality which exists only as it is created by those in the society whose interests are served by its presence.
6. Criminal and noncriminal behavior stem from people acting rationally in ways that are compatible with their class position. Crime is a reaction to the life conditions of a person's social class.

Chambliss and Seidman presented an analysis of the legal order which was clearly based in conflict theory. Theirs was a Marxian view of society that saw the powerful influence of the justice bureaucracy. Later Chambliss emphasized the impact of the economic substructure on the bureaucracy. The transition has been in the direction of a stronger Marxism view, which has been labeled *Critical Criminology*.

Critical Criminology

The term "critical criminology" has been subjected to general application by some who fail to recognize the somewhat subtle distinctions involved. One contemporary criminologist (Sykes, 1974:212) gives a correct portrayal of the Critical Criminology as a perspective: "It forces an inquiry into precisely how the normative content of the criminal law is internalized in different segments of society, and how norm-holding is actually related to behavior." In a very mild form this is Critical Criminology. Unfortunately, all of the recent alternatives to traditional criminology have been conveniently grouped under the term "critical criminology" (Sykes, 1974:206-213).

Marvin Wolfgang (1973:18) viewed Critical Criminology as that school of thought which seeks to maintain an alliance with the system—social, political, and economic—while criticizing, and even attacking, the system for its failure to promote social justice. Wolfgang astutely terms the Critical Criminology perspective as "more reactive than proactive" (1973:18). It is aimed at recognizing faults through critical analysis. Richard Quinney, the foremost critical criminologist, gave an excellent example of this perspective when, during a discussion with Austin Turk, Quinney stated that he was critical of all theories, including critical theories (1977).

Another criminologist, whose work serves as an excellent example of the Critical Criminology, is Barry Krisberg. Though Krisberg is correctly classified as a radical criminologist, a statement in *Crime and Privilege* perfectly fits the critical analysis of crime and criminality (1975:5):

> The New Criminology directs us to ask basic questions about the quality of justice in our society; it asks us to evaluate the democracy of our political institutions, the fairness of our economic institutions, and the humanity of our social relationships.

Quinney maintains that critical analyses allow one to slip into another existence and survey his own as well as other perspectives in an effort to gain a realization of how things could be (1977:25). "A critical philosophy lets us break with the ideology of the age, for built into critical thinking is the ability to think negatively" (Quinney, 1975:13).

Quinney maintains that Critical Criminology is synonymous with new criminology since "seeking a critical understanding and questioning the legal system have traditionally fallen outside the dominant ideological and scientific interest of most criminologists" (1975:13). Quinney is most certainly viewing criminology and all of society from a Marxian perspective. He states: "If any body of thought has a notion of truth and beauty, of how things could be, it is that of Marxism" (1975:25). Given this focus, it can be expected that his analysis of the crime problem will involve the subjects of capitalism, classes, and the law as an instrument of oppression.

Three of Quinney's most recent books, *Critique of Legal Order* (1973), *Criminology* (1975), and *Class, State, and Crime* (1977) reflect the key ingredients to his critical analysis and theory.

In *Critique of Legal Order,* Quinney devotes the first

chapter to a critique of criminological theories. He classifies criminological approaches or modes of analysis in four categories: (1) the *positivistic;* (2) the *social constructionist;* (3) the *phenomenological;* and (4) the *critical.* The positivistic mode is concerned only with developing methods to "discover" what external phenomena are responsible for criminal behavior. Quinney maintains (1973:2-4) that this mode of analysis is so myoptic that it fails to recognize the power relations in a capitalistic society as influencing factors in the reality of crime.

In his consideration of the social constructionist approach, Quinney says that while it is more "reflexive" than positivism, it still does not allow the researcher to analyze reality by holding it up to the ideal of human justice as opposed to legal order. Therefore, this mode of analysis tends to ignore those conditions in society that cause repression and alienation (1973:5-8). Phenomenology, as a mode of analysis, defines reality as experience where no prior knowledge is assumed. While this is favored over the two approaches discussed previously because it allows the researcher to "move toward a transcendence of our experience," it still is not fully critical so as to allow a total transcendence of the existing order (1973:10). Quinney summarizes his critique of the three dominant modes of analyzing crime as being inadequate (1973:15):

> Positivists have regarded law as a natural mechanism, social constructionists have regarded it relativistically, as one of man's conveniences and even the phenomenologists, though examining underlying assumptions, have done little to provide or promote an alternative existence.

Early in the book Quinney outlines his critical theory of criminal law (1973:16):

1. American society is based on an advanced capitalist economy.
2. The state is organized to serve the interests of the dominant economic class, the capitalist ruling class.
3. Criminal law is an instrument that the state and dominant ruling

class use to maintain and perpetuate the social and economic order.
4. Crime control in capitalist society is accomplished by a governmental elite, representing dominant ruling class interests, to establish domestic order.
5. The contradictions of advanced capitalism—the disjunction between existence and essence—require that the subordinate classes remain oppressed by whatever means necessary, especially by the legal system's coercion and violence.
6. Only with the collapse of capitalist society, based on socialist principles, will there be a solution to the crime problem.

With respect to the fact that American society is based on a capitalist economy, Quinney asserts that his critique begins with the assumption that life in the United States is a product of and determined by the capitalist mode of production. The division between the rulers and the ruled in capitalistic societies "establishes the nature of political, economic, and social life in [those societies]."

The second proposition holds that the state is organized to serve the interests of the dominant class (1973:51):

> The state is thus a political organization created out of force and coercion. The state is established by those who desire to protect their material basis and who have the power (because of material means) to maintain the state. The law in capitalist society gives political recognition to powerful interests (1973:52).

Quinney's view of the "ruling class" is a strict Marxian view. The ruling class is seen as "that class which owns and controls the means of production and which is able, by virtue of the economic power thus conferred upon it, to use the state as its instrument for the domination of society" (1973:53).

Quinney maintains that the criminal law is an instrument of the state and ruling class to maintain and perpetuate the existing social and economic order. In order to understand the composition and policy of the criminal law, the class composition of those who formulate the criminal law must be critically examined. Such an examination yields the fact that, according to Quinney, crime commissions, legislative bodies, crime control bureaucracies, and advisory groups all "operate to preserve domestic order for the ruling class" (1973:59). The capitalist order, represented by the agencies of control, determine who or what groups pose threats to the order and the dominant economic class. Those who pose political threats are then labeled criminals because they are threats to domestic security. "The rates of crime in any state are an indication of the extent to which the ruling class, through its machinery of criminal law, must coerce the rest of the population, thereby preventing any threats to its ability to rule and possess" (1973:52).

The fourth proposition concerns the accomplishment of crime control. Quinney states that it "is accomplished by institutions and agencies established and administered by a governmental elite, representing dominant ruling class interests, to establish domestic order" (1973:16). After examining the background and composition of the agencies and agents of control in America, Quinney concludes (1973:88-89):

> Their interests and the interests of those they serve are basically the same. The sincere purpose is to control behavior and activity that will threaten the existing order. Hence, those who create crime control agencies and those who manage them are united in a common cause. The crime control bureaucracies and the men within them conform to a pattern: law and order in the name of preserving domestic order.

Crime control serves only the interests of the dominant economic class rather than the interests of the society. In order to discuss the law as something other than that which perpetuates the ruling class, legislators "are in basic agreement on the control, through law, of behavior and activities that threaten the capitalist system—euphemistically referred to as 'the American way of life'." (1973:100).

The fifth proposition is that the contradictions of advanced capitalism require that the subordinate classes remain oppressed by whatever means necessary, especially by the legal system's coercion and violence. The contradictions of capitalism refer to the contention that there is "a dialectic in the development of capitalism." It produces forces that contribute to the construction and advance of capitalism, yet are "at the same time destructive to the advances of capitalism. ... For every advance in capitalism there is also generated a force that opposes this advance" (1973:166). The opposing forces are subjected to the coercion of the law and the legal order in an effort to maintain tranquility while maintaining capitalism. The more frequently the repressive apparatus of the state is aimed at those who struggle against capitalism, the more likely the demise of capitalism becomes. "Crime is thus caused by capitalism and it is capitalism that will assure the continuation of the crime problem. To remove the apparatus that coerces and defines the oppressed as criminal, would be to destroy the capitalist system" (1973:168). A very simplistic, but accurate, synopsis of Quinney's theory is that capitalism produces crime.

A discussion of the ways in which capitalistic society responds to its own "contradictions" includes an interesting analysis of "reforms." Reforms take on the status of adaptive mechanisms, but they are actually designed to accommodate the capitalist system itself. For example, up until the early 1970s, the correctional system had as its role the rehabilitation of offenders. And in Quinney's words, "prisons [are] to be made into therapeutic centers, where offenders will be scientifically *managed* and *manipulated,* and finally reintegrated into society" (1973:183). [Emphasis added.]

The last proposition states that only with the collapse of capitalist society and the creation of a new society, based on socialist principles, will there be a solution to the crime problem:

> With the achievement of a socialist society, devoid of classes, bureaucracy, and centralized authority ... the state may no longer be necessary ... there may be no state law. Law as we know it today will be relegated to the history of a former age. (1973:190)

This does not imply that crime will cease, but that the repressive control agencies that are the chief perpetrators of crime will disappear.

As a textbook of criminological theory, Quinney's *Crimi-*

nology is refreshing in that it provides a radically different method of examining traditional points of view. In this work, his theoretical basis of Conflict Criminology is set forth.

Quinney developed a theory which he presented in 1970, and revised in 1975, called the *social reality of crime*. This theory is made up of six propositions, each of which will be discussed separately.

The first proposition concerns the definition of crime (1975:37): "Crime as a legal definition of human conduct is created by agents of the dominant class in a politically organized society." Crime is not studied behaviorally but is considered to be a definition of behavior which is conferred on some by those in positions of power. "Crime, according to this first proposition, is not inherent in behavior but is a judgment made by some about the actions and characteristics of others" (1975:37). By beginning with this proposition, Quinney is basing his focus not on those who bear the label *criminal*, but on those who confer the label—the *dominant class*.

The second proposition refers to the formulation of definitions of crime. "Definitions of crime are composed of behaviors that conflict with the interests of the dominant class" (1975:38). The law represents the interests of the dominant class; therefore, the definitions of crime represent those who are able to translate their interests into public policy. Quinney contends that the interests of the powerful are reflected by the procedural elements of legal policies in handling those who have been defined as criminals. The interests of those in power are also reflected in the definitions of substantive criminal law. In a succinct and cynical statement Quinney says (1975:38):

> From the initial definitions of crime to the subsequent procedures, correctional and penal programs, and policies for controlling and preventing crime, those who have the power regulate the behavior of those without the power.

The third proposition relates to the application of the definitions of crime (1975:38): "Definitions of crime are applied by the class that has the power to shape the enforcement and administration of criminal law." Quinney traces the presence and prevalence of dominant interests in every stage of the crime-related process. He maintains that if the interests of some conflict with those of the powerful, the less powerful must either change their behavior or risk the possibility of having the label of criminal applied to their behavior. The probability that the label will be applied varies according to the degree to which the behavior of the less powerful conflicts with the interests of the dominant class. The dominant class does not physically apply the criminal law. They delegate this authority to their "legal agents." This, according to Quinney, is what is responsible for varying levels of enforcement and emphasis. "Because the groups responsible for creating the definitions of crime are physically separated from the groups that have the authority to enforce and administer law, local conditions determine how the definitions will be applied" (1975:38).

The fourth proposition refers to how behavior patterns develop in relation to definitions of crime (1975:39). "Behavior patterns are structured in relation to definitions of crime, and within this context people engage in actions that have relative probabilities of being defined as criminal." Quinney seems to be following Turk's analysis of criminalization (Turk, 1966:34) in saying that it is not the quality of the behavior, but the perception of the person—and the class—as offensive or inoffensive, that determines whether or not the definition of criminal will be applied; those whose behavior patterns conflict with those of the dominant class stand a great chance to be eventually defined as criminal:

> Thus, both the definers of crime and the criminally defined are involved in reciprocal action patterns. The personal action patterns of both the definers and the defined are shared by their common, continued, and related experiences. The fate of each is bound to that of the other (Quinney, 1975:39).

The fifth proposition of the social reality of crime concerns the construction of an ideology of crime (1975:39). "An ideology of crime is constructed and diffused by the dominant class to secure its hegemony." The factors that determine the ideology of an individual are the ideas to which he is exposed, the manner of selecting information to fit his environment, and the way he interprets this information. "People behave in reference to the *social meanings* they attach to their experiences" (1975:39). These social meanings are assigned by the dominant class by controlling the information meted out to the subordinate class.

The last proposition is the construction of the social reality of crime (1975:40): "The social reality of crime is constructed by the formulation and application of definitions of crime, the development of behavior patterns in relation to these definitions, and the construction of an ideology of crime." This proposition is a composite of the previous five. Quinney states (1975:40):

> The theory of the social reality of crime, accordingly, postulates creating a series of phenomena that increase the probability of crime. The result, holistically, is the social reality of crime.

All of the elements of the social reality of crime interact with each other as well as with the presence of class struggles and class conflict to "culminate in what is regarded as the amount and character of crime at any time" (1975:41).

In his most recent book (1977) Quinney considers the criminal justice system and critically analyzes it as to theory and practice in society. He begins his discussion by stating (1977:v):

> Criminal Justice has emerged as a principal feature or modern, advanced capitalist society. When a society cannot solve the social problems of its own creation, policies for the control of the population must be devised and implemented. The purpose of this book is to understand the meaning of criminal justice in theory and practice as found in the United States.

In his book, Quinney seems to consolidate his previous ideas and theories and apply them to the practice of criminal justice. He states (1977:1): "justice begins in contradiction." This contradiction is between the ideal—"justice transcends everyday existence"—and the practice of criminal justice—"justice is inevitably shaped by social reality." The result is that "justice is rarely realized."

Justice in a capitalistic society is seen as difficult to accomplish and it becomes progressively more difficult as the classes become more instilled and the gap between the interests becomes greater. Quinney reviews the proliferation of crime repressing (therefore subordinate class-suppressing) programs in the United States since the mid-1960s. An interesting observation, which indicates Quinney's orientation, is in the area of the Citizen Initiative Programs of the Law Enforcement Assistance Administration (LEAA). Though Quinney characterizes the LEAA as one of the giant arms of the state in developing and continuing means of repression and control, he sees the citizens' programs, which are intended to increase autonomy and self-sufficiency in the area of crime prevention, as a part of the dialectic which reflects the contradictions of capitalist legal order. He predicts that as the citizens' groups gain participation outside the state's control, they will increasingly be seen as threats and therefore, "community actions themselves will be subject to criminal justice" (1973:13).

Criminal justice is failing to control the populace. New techniques are being proposed; yet they are failing. This, according to Quinney, represents weaknesses in the capitalistic structure of our society. The failure of criminal justice and implications this has for capitalism calls for society to move beyond its present social and political economy. "The final development of capitalism is also the initial development of socialism. Thus, as criminal justice falters with the development of capitalism, new socialist forms of justice emerge" (Quinney, 1977:145). These forms of justice are termed "popular justice" and are intended to "project and solidify the working class against internal and external enemies, as well as against elitist bureaucratic tendencies in the state apparatus" (1977:163).

It is not the intention of this discussion to evaluate the specific points of Quinney's theories, but to use them as examples, the most prominent examples, of Critical Criminology. Quinney states (1975:291):

> As we develop a critical imagination, we are thinking about things that have never appeared to us. Where will a critical theory of crime lead? It will take us to places where no one has been. In thought and action, we are entering new realms of life, imagination, and human possibility.

The New Criminology (1975) by Ian Taylor, Paul Walton, and Jock Young is placed in the category of Critical Criminology even though the authors tend to see themselves as "radical criminologists" (Taylor and Young, 1978). Alvin Gouldner said of the book (Taylor et al., 1973:ix): "It is perhaps the first truly comprehensive critique that we have ever had of the totality, of past and contemporary, of European and American, studies of 'crime' and 'deviance'." It is in this context that the work is seen as an example of Critical Criminology.

Taylor, Walton, and Young indicate in the first chapter of their book that the theory they are formulating is a social theory that transcends positivism (1973:30):

> We shall attempt, as the argument in this book evolves, to show that a fully social theory of deviance would be rather more demanding and comprehensive an explanation than that which is required in positivism.

Later, they comment (1973:66), "Our position in this critique is not one in which psychology is totally excluded or denied ... the most pressing need is for social psychology which is capable of situating the actions of men according to beliefs and values in their historical and structural contexts."

In the third chapter, the authors deal with Durkheim and his influence in the study of crime and delinquency. There is obvious respect for Durkheim and his break with tradition.

He is characterized as "unambiguously radical in his approach to social order" (1973:87) and as one who developed a "radical politicality" in the sociology of deviance (1973:89). In discussing recent British contributions to explanations of crime and delinquency, the authors state (1973:118-119):

> They have broken with the tendency to reduce what is in reality a number of overlapping and sometimes contradictory systems of social relations ... to a monolithic culture where deviants are seen as pathological blemishes on the otherwise perfectible and integrated whole. This has opened up the possibility of a theory which can encompass change, conflict, and struggle....

Taylor, Walton, and Young also survey the contributions of Marx, Engels, and Bonger to theories of social control. They seem to see all three as having made tremendous advances in defining the correct variables to be considered; yet, they do not totally agree with any of those theorists considered. They indicate that their theory would "involve a model—suggested but not followed thoroughly by Marx himself—of the dialectics of human action . . ." (1973:236).

The authors' assessment of the *new conflict theorist* (1973:237-267) presents an introduction to the realm of the alternative to the consensual view of society:

> The challenges made by 'the new conflict theorists' to the paradigmatic theories of structural functionalism, appear to have been prompted, not so much by a reexamination of the classical social theorists, but rather by events in the real world which have thrown the assumption of 'consensus' into doubt (1973:237).

The discussion considers the points of view of Vold, Dahrendorf, Turk, and Quinney. In general, the theories and perspectives are seen as "not especially new" in that these criminologists fail to view man as the purposive creator of action (1973:266-267). They maintain that the "new conflict theorists" continue to stress that criminal behavior is determined and the criminal man is pathological (1973:267).

Predictably, the authors have an alternative to all of the existing theories, one in which man is seen as a purposive being. Their alternative contains all of the formal and substantive requirements of a fully social theory of deviance. The following is a synopsis of those formal requirements of the theory (1973:270-278):

1. *A Political Economy of Crime.* [An adequately social theory] must be able to place the [deviant] act in terms of its wider structural origins.
2. *A Social Psychology of Crime.* [The theory] must be able to explain the different events, experiences, or structural developments that precipitate the deviant act.
3. *The Social Dynamics of the Act.* [The theory] must be able to explain the relationship between beliefs and action, between the optimum 'rationality' that men have chosen and the behaviors they actually carry through.
4. *A Social Psychology of Social Reaction.* The theory must offer an explanation of the immediate reaction of the social audience in terms of the range of choices available to that audience.
5. *A Political Economy of Social Reaction.* [The theory] must present an effective model of the political and economic imperatives that underpin "lay ideologies" as well as the "crusades" which emerge to control or alter the amount and level of deviance.
6. *The Outcome of the Social Reaction on Deviant's Further Action.* A social explanation of deviance would be one in which the deviant actor is always endowed with some degree of consciousness about the likelihood and consequences of reaction against him, and his subsequent decisions are developed from that initial degree of consciousness.
7. *The Scope of Theoretical Analysis.* A social theory of deviance must present all of these formal requirements as they appear in the real world, that is, in a complex, dialectical relationship to one another.

The authors have laid claim to formulating the ingredients of a social theory of deviance; yet they have not formulated the theory itself. They are to be commended for specifying the multitudinous areas which must be taken into consideration in developing a theory which, they argue, would "move criminology out of its own imprisonment in artificially segregated specifics, and bring the parts together again in order to form the whole" (1973:279).

In a later publication (1975a), Taylor, Walton, and Young

admit the inchoate complexion of the New Criminology (1975a:20-21):

> *The New Criminology* was (implicitly) an exercise in radical critique in a way that crucially distinguishes it from conservative and liberal texts in the same area of discussion.

Yet, in the same publication, and in spite of the title *Critical Criminology,* Taylor, Walton, and Young indicate that they have gone beyond a critical analysis of crime and deviance and now advocate the *change* they feel is necessary to abolish crime (1975b:20):

> Albeit by implication, the insistence in *The New Criminology* was that, insofar as the crime-producing features of contemporary capitalism are bound up with the inequities and divisions in material production and ownership, then it must be possible via social transformations to create social and productive arrangements that would abolish crime.

Critical Criminology, as discussed here, provides a framework for evaluating traditional criminology. In this regard it would more appropriately be termed "exposé criminology." This is basically the criminology engaged in by Taylor, Walton, and Young in *The New Criminology.* Quinney utilized exposé criminology in evaluating traditional theories and perspectives, but also constructed what he considered realistic theories of deviance and criminality. The critical criminologists seem to have gone farther from "theory" than conflict criminologists and closer to *praxis*. It is in the Radical School of Criminology that theory is almost totally disregarded, except as something to criticize, and radical *methods* are seen as optimum.

Both critical and radical criminologists use the method of *critique*. As Gouldner states, critiques of theory show how "the theory relates to and serves the larger society, especially the leading elites, and ... how this relationship has shaped the theory itself" (1973:427-428). Gouldner seems to be voicing the opinion of both Quinney and the Taylor, Walton, and Young group when he states (1973:429):

A critique, then, aims at making men's potency more fully manifest so that men might then make their own history—consciously rather than blindly. A natural science, in contrast, will, by providing laws that presumably determine the human will, allow those having technical knowledge of these laws to apply their knowledge in a technological way and to formulate the problem of social change as a *technical* problem.

The goal of Critical Criminology seems to be the demystification of criminology, the legal order, and criminal justice. Radical Criminology extends the critique and follows Marx in viewing criticism "not as a lancet but a weapon. Its object is an *enemy* which it aims not to refute but to destroy.... Criticism is no longer an end in itself, but simply a means; *indignation* is its essential mode of feeling, and denunciation its principal task" (Bottomore, 1963:46). Radical criminologists utilize the critical method; but it is a minor portion of their endeavor. Their *raison d'etre* is *praxis*. This becomes evident in the review of Radical Criminology.

Radical Criminology

"Radical Criminology draws primarily from the critical theory ... [which] ultimately exposes the oppression of the existing reality and makes us live in a way [through action and thought] to remove that oppression—creating a new world" (Johnson, 1978:11-12). The key to understanding Radical Criminology seems to be the emphasis on change, practice, and *praxis*. It is based heavily in Marxian theory for "in the Marxian view, social science should subordinate theory to practice...." (Hodges, 1970:91).

Radical Criminology is a fairly new crime-related discipline. Johnson recognizes that "because the movement has surfaced rather recently, even the opponents are likely to recognize that time and energy must be expended in the elaboration and development of new ideas" (1978:3). For this reason examples of Radical Criminology must be constructed from the contributions of several sources.

Herman Schwendinger wrote in 1974 that Radical Criminology was beginning to emerge in academic criminology in the United States, but that it was confined to a "small number of outspoken students and a smaller number of determined faculty. ... The number involved, however, should not minimize the qualitative significance of the development of a Radical Criminology" (1974:1).

In the same issue of a journal of Radical Criminology, Tony Platt commented that radical scholarship involving university-trained intellectuals is not highly developed due mainly to an absence of a Marxian tradition. He states (1974:2):

> The roots of this radicalism are to be found in political struggles—the civil rights movement, the anti-war movement, the student movement, third world liberation struggles inside as well as outside the United States, and anti-imperialist movements—and in the writings of participants in these struggles—George Jackson (1970), Angela Davis (1971), Eldridge Cleaver (1968), Tom Hayden (1970), Sam Melville (1971), Bobby Seale (1968), Huey Newton (1973), Malcolm X (1964) and Rucheu Magee, to name a few.

This attitude consciously or subconsciously subordinates theory and intellectualism to practice and revolution.

The prospects for a Radical Criminology, according to radical criminologists themselves, involve a "self-critical analysis of criminology's development during the last hundred years as well as discovering continuities in earlier radical traditions in the United States" (Platt, 1974:5). In this regard *The New Criminology* (Taylor, Walton, and Young, 1973) is seen as a major effort to analyze the past. Another major characteristic of Radical Criminology is "a re-definition of subject matter, concerns, and commitments" (Platt, 1974:5). This involves a redefinition of crime departing from the legal definition and the recognition that the reality of a legal system is that it is based on power and privilege. Platt states (1974:6) that there is also a need for the development of "an analysis of the relationship between the criminal justice system and other sectors of the state apparatus, federal policy and strategy, of the organization and ideology of the criminal justice system labor force, or the illegal marketplace" and the political functions of corrections, prisoners, and control of the police (Platt, 1974:6). The final ingredient Platt discusses is the realization that for there to be a radical theory of criminology there must be a commitment to "practical critical activity and participation in ongoing political struggles" (1974:6). The specific methods include participating in political struggles "by organizing educational conferences, supporting defendants in political trials, participating in campus protests, and helping to develop programs such as community control of the police" (Platt, 1974:7). This sets the stage for *praxis*—which is what sets Radical Criminology apart from other perspectives.

The arena for the development of all the other perspectives discussed in this book is academe. It is within the academic institution that perspectives are evaluated, tested, negated or approved. Yet Radical Criminology, because of its emphasis on practice, seems to be ambivalent to the use of the university as a breeding ground for the perspective. But Platt contends that radical criminologists should "begin within our own workplace and with what we know best—the university" (Platt, 1974:7). Yet a Canadian radical criminologist states (Dandurand, 1975:49):

> In Canada, as in the United States, the radical approach to criminology appeared in the community at large and among those active in the 'struggle for justice' long before it did within academia. And even to this day, the latter has not contributed very much to the movement.

Perhaps some view academia as not taking an "active" role in Radical Criminology because of the emphasis on *praxis*. Paul Takagi, when asked about the role of the academician in furthering the cause of Radical Criminology, states (1978):

> We get more benefit from miners striking and other things that bring attention to the inequities of the political system than from the universities. Radical criminologists cannot seem to find jobs in university programs.

It is not *praxis*—the interrelationship between theory and practice—that is denounced by critics of Radical Criminology. Elmer Johnson indicates (1978:4-6) that the concept of *science-oriented praxis* strengthens science and strengthens theory; yet "in departing from science-oriented praxis, American radical criminologists have sought to gain allies through strategic action based on 'anti-correctionalism'" which "breaks the theory-practice linkage" and plunges "Radical Criminology into the swamp of subjectivism" (Johnson, 1978:6). *Praxis* can be a tool of construction or destruction. Johnson maintains (1978:8-9):

> When a genuine linkage between theory and practice exists, *praxis* holds promise for realizing the potential of scientific Marxism for further development of theoretical criminology. Although conceptually distinct from the usual liberal conception of the need to relate theory and practice, *praxis* invites a detached reexamination of 'value-free' theory, the relevance of 'enlightenment' in 'new consciousness' in narrowing discrepancies between criminal justice and contemporary mores without the narrow purposes of 'strategic action' and the intellectual merits of serious Marxist scholarship.

It is how the concept of *praxis* is employed that some criminologists find objectionable. If it is perceived by them that radical criminologists employ *praxis* for revolutionary purposes only, it could easily be viewed as threatening and anti- or extra-scientific.

The legal definition of crime is one of the major points of concern of new criminologists; but the ideology of the radical criminologists advocates the abandonment of the legal definition. "Most criminologists assume a state definition of crime, taking as their initial reference point the legal code as the subject matter of investigation and analysis" (Platt, 1974:2). Radical criminologists not only find this concern with legally defined and prosecuted criminals as disagreeable but contend that it reflects and reenforces the values of the state. They contend that this is an effort on the part of the state to mystify and cloud the fact that the major "crimes" against society are committed by the state (American Friends Service Committee, 1971:10-11):

Actions that clearly ought to be labeled 'criminal,' because they bring the greatest harm to the greatest number, are in fact accomplished officially by agencies of government. The overwhelming number of murders in this century has been committed by governments in wartime. Hundreds of unlawful killings by police go unprosecuted each year. The largest forceful acquisitions of property in the United States have been the theft of lands guaranteed by treaty to Indian tribes, thefts sponsored by the government. The largest number of dislocations, tantamount to kidnapping—the evacuation and internment of Japanese-Americans during World War II—was carried out by the government with the approval of the courts. Civil rights demonstrators, struggling to exercise their constitutional rights, have been repeatedly beaten and harassed by police and sheriffs. And in the Vietnam War, America has violated its constitution and international law.

In an effort to formulate a definition of crime that reflects the reality of the law as based on power and privilege, Herman and Julia Schwendinger (1975) proposed a radical view of the law that would define crime as a violation of politically defined human rights (1975:134):

> Criminologists must be able to identify those [criminal] forms of individuals' behavior and social institutions which should be engaged in order to defend human rights. To defend human rights, criminologists must be able to sufficiently identify the violations of these rights—by whom and against whom; and how and why.

This represents a reconstruction of the definition of crime which allows the examination of sexism, imperialism, capitalism, racism, and other means of exploitation that "contribute to human misery and deprive people of their human potentiality" (Platt, 1974:6).

Radical criminologists call not only for a demasking of the moral and ideological veneer of "liberal criminology" and an unequal society, but also for the institution of methods to remove the unbearable conditions of capitalism and imperialism. These radical criminologists obviously represent the extreme version of criminology.

Criticisms of the New Criminology

In addition to differences of opinion between and among the

proponents of the New Criminology, articles and comments in opposition to the perspective are beginning to surface. Some criticisms are based on the evaluation that the "New Criminology" is not new but is simply a restatement of the old. Other critics indicate that the perspective is formed on an erroneous platform, while others tend to believe that the New Criminology is an exercise in futility. Yet it must be acknowledged that criticism is a healthy element in any scientific endeavor because it causes the perspective being criticized to be sharpened by its defense and reshaped if necessary.

Elmer H. Johnson recently examined the ideological underpinnings of the New Criminology (1977). In his comment he delineated the types of "skepticism" involved in any scientific endeavor. One type is the "skepticism of science which subjects all ideas to relentless and inclusive investigation in the pursuit of truth, regardless of personal preference, private belief, or ingrained habit" (1977:1). This is the approach of an objective, value-free science which Johnson implies is present in traditional criminology. Johnson contends that the other type of skepticism is reflected by the new perspective (1977:1-2):

> Rather than engaging in the testing of all perspectives, including one's own, partisanship colors the rebel's negativistic rejection of the total existing order or the apologist's defense of that order. 'Facts' and 'theories' are utilized selectively for the purpose of gaining ascendancy over opponents, rather than to extend the range of verified information and reliable principles.

Johnson views the contribution of the New Criminology as being limited to the " 'gadfly' functions of negativistic, partisan skepticism" (1974:4). Further, he finds that the New Criminology which is presumed to be synonymous with Marxist Criminology, presents serious difficulties in the exchange of "skepticism" between non-Marxists and the new criminologists. That which is accepted as given by some is severely questioned by others. This is evident in the monolythic view of Taylor, Walton, and Young that the study of crime must be fully social and not "blighted" by non-social assumptions (1973:268-270).

In recent correspondence (1978), Johnson has candidly given his impression of the new perspective:

> Although I do not regard myself as an expert on 'New Criminology,' I have found its more worthy advocates to be very useful in pointing out the weaknesses and ideological agenda latent in the so-called "liberal criminology." I have gained genuine intellectual profit by being pressed to reexamine my earlier naive acceptance of the liberal rhetoric in my service as a prison executive, university professor, and researcher.

In this statement, Johnson seems to be indicating that the New Criminology is useful in the role of a "devil's advocate," but due to the lack of evidence of a truly adequate theoretical perspective within the New Criminology, he is hesitant to embrace its propositions.

Another who questioned the contribution of Taylor, Walton, and Young's *The New Criminology* posits that the book seems to lead to "intellectual clouds which will generate more heat than light" (Hackler, 1977:192). This critic maintains that *The New Criminology* is useful as a tool of critique but does not clarify assumptions or advance ideas that are testable. "The authors also seem very reluctant to accept contributions made by .others or to view them as stepping stones to more adequate explanation" (Hackler, 1977:192).

A more general criticism of the New Criminology as a perspective was made by David Greenberg (1977). He maintained that the proponents of the New Criminology have ignored the consensus of the public concerning many categories of crime. He also cited the fact that many crimes are committed by underprivileged individuals on others in similar circumstances, thus negating the contention that all crimes are crimes of capitalism and domination

One of the most impressive critiques of the New Criminology is by Jackson Toby (1977). He begins with the assertion that "the New Criminology is not new. It draws upon an old tradition of sentimentality toward those who break social rules" (1977:1). He discounts as gross sentimentality the contention that the poor are compelled to steal because they are hungry. He states (1977:1), "Color television sets and automobiles are stolen more often than food and blankets."

Toby discusses two "myths" that the New Criminology views as domain assumptions. The first myth is the contention of discriminatory law enforcement. The New Criminology holds that one of the reasons crime takes place in underprivileged areas more often than in affluent areas is due to discriminatory law enforcement. This myth is discounted by Toby logically and empirically by the fact that the major factor in police response is the seriousness of the act. On theoretical grounds, the fact that persons from lower socioeconomic levels contribute disproportionately to crime is explained by social stratification:

> Higher social status means better life chances; lower social status means poorer life chances. Life chances for what? Among nonmaterial advantages children from higher social strata enjoy is the greater likelihood of being socialized in a stable family which includes the same cultural values embodied in the criminal law (1977:4).

The person whose socioeconomic background is reflective of the higher social strata is most likely to want to conform to accepted behavior.

The other myth attacked by Toby is that of the prominence of white-collar crime, which he characterizes as "an assumption of middle-class immorality" (1977:5). The New Criminology would have one believe that since the emphasis of criminal statistics is on the "garden variety of crimes," the incidence of criminality in the lower class is an illusion intended to hide the fact that if white-collar crimes were recorded as diligently, it would be obvious that crime is just as prevalent in high places. Toby points out that it is "theoretically sloppy to assume that only white-collar persons commit crimes in the course of their occupational activities (what about the dishonest garage mechanic?) and that middle-class persons do not engage in "ordinary" crime (don't middle-class persons commit murder, rape, and assault?)" (1977:6).

Toby closes his argument with the point that it is dangerous to discount *or* exaggerate crime at any one level of society:

> Some criminologists are too ready to discount sin in low places and unduly prone to exaggerate the incidence of sin in high places. Criminality and immorality occur on every social level, but the likelihood is that the relatively disadvantaged contribute disproportionately to the crime rate.

The critiques of the New Criminology seem to center on the book by Taylor, Walton, and Young (1973) or on the radical perspective. It is unfortunate that the critics have done exactly what Toby accused the radical criminologists of "throwing the baby out with the bath water to abandon all attempts to distinguish deviant from acceptable behavior" (1971:12)—yet, by not distinguishing between the acceptable and unacceptable propositions within the New Criminology perspective, the critics are discounting the complete range of propositions. The purpose of the detailed evaluation and separation of the positions within the New Criminology was to allow opponents to be more selective in opposition rather than abandoning the entire perspective.

Conclusion: The Future of Criminology

The New Criminology, whether seen to be "conflict," "critical," or "radical," represents a marked departure from the traditional criminology. The propositions of Vold and Turk discussed in the Conflict Criminology portion of this book closely resemble the ideology of the labelling theorists of traditional criminology; therefore, the conflict perspective represents the point on the continuum of the New Criminology which is the closest to the more traditional points of view. Conflict theorists are very much involved in the theoretical aspects of criminology. This does not indicate, however, that they are not concerned with *praxis* or "action." Turk (1975:42) agrees with radicals on the utility of *praxis* in furthering the New Criminology; yet, he disagrees on the "how" involved. Though oriented toward change and application, conflict theorists are more concerned with gradual, long-term, "publicly acceptable" action. In this regard they could be termed *active intellectuals*.

Critical criminologists also favor *praxis* and focus on it more than conflict theorists but less than radical criminologists. Quinney (1977:159) points out that a necessary element to the socialist revolution is "real, living, human beings struggling against the oppressive conditions of capitalism." This involves the exposure of oppressive conditions, using the critical method, and also the struggle itself—*praxis*. He continues (1977:160): "Theory without practice not only makes bad theory but also shuts off the possibility of actual political struggle." Theory is seen as the catalytic agent, therefore the focal concern is still on theory. But proponents of the New Criminology do not discount the necessity for action. Critical criminologists could, therefore, be labeled *intellectual activists*. Even though they are often not engaged in active revolutionary practices, they recognize the validity of these methods for change. Richard Quinney remarked (1978) that he has been criticized by some because he has not actively engaged in revolutionary practices. He states that he counters that criticism with the remark that Marx was a writer and thinker, not an *active* revolutionary.

Radical criminologists view *praxis* as more important than science or theory. They view "intellectualism" as a negative quality due to the "academic repression" and "elitism" associated with intellectuals. Practice is then the most important factor in the struggle to replace capitalism with socialism. In this vein, radical criminologists can be labeled as *active activists*.

Though these labels—active intellectuals, intellectual activists, and active activists—are simplistic and subsume a great deal of qualifying comments concerning the theorists' individual idiosyncracies, they are used to indicate the major variance in the points of the continuum of the new criminology. Where the conflict theorists subordinate practice to theory, the radicals subordinate theory to practice, with the critical criminologists seemingly emphasizing both.

This inverse relationship seems to also be present in the concern over the legal definition of crime. Conflict criminologists, again represented by Turk (1975:41), state that the legalistic definitions of crimes have promoted neglect of serious offenses linked with the dominant interest groups, but that there should not be a "total rejection of the state-crime link." Critical criminologists, true to the nature of critical analysis, call for a reanalysis and reconsideration of the legal order: "Everything we have done in criminology and the sociology of law has to be redone" (Quinney, 1974:143). Radical criminologists—again the extreme—call for a junking of the legal definition of crime and the birth of a "human rights" orientation.

The arena of the struggle for the New Criminology also varies among the perspectives. Turk argues that what is needed is "not some escape from the constraints of scientific pragmatism, but an authentic acceptance of them" (Turk, 1975:42). Academe should not be abandoned but fertilized so as to generate the theory construction necessary to provide an adequate or optimum model of where we should go. To do otherwise, Turk says, is to increase the opposition (1975:42):

> I am arguing for a classic liberal notion that 'there are many ways to skin a cat' and for a modern labeling notion that people who are attacked and rejected as cop sociologists, government finks, bird-brained liberal thinkers, etc., are not only denied enlightenment but driven toward even more stubborn adherence to the 'roles' to which they are considered.

Quinney (1975:13) finds that criminologists are presently "ancilliary agents of political power" but through critical understanding a truly "new criminology" can be developed which will allow the existence of a critical life. Radical criminologists view the academic environment as repressive and unfruitful, and though they must operate within it in order to acquaint others with their plight, they find it ridden with repression and attempts at cooptation (Marzotto, Platt, and Snare, 1975:43).

Despite the variations of thought and emphasis within the domain, the New Criminology can be regarded as nothing less than revolutionary. And the fact that this emerging perspective has gained the knowledge of dedicated criminologists throughout the country reflects a remarkable commitment to change—to a critical repositioning in the study of the social, political, and economic dynamics of crime and its control. Finally, as Quinney says (1975:291):

To think critically and radically today is to be revolutionary. To do otherwise is to concede to oppression.

References

Abrahamsen, D. *The psychology of crime.* New York: Columbia University Press, 1960.

Allen, F. Raffaele Garofalo. In Herman Mannheim (ed.), *Pioneers in criminology.* Marion: Patterson Smith, 1972.

American Friends Service Committee. *Struggle for justice.* New York: Hill and Wang, 1971.

Barnes, H. E., & Teeters, N. K. *New horizons in criminology.* New York: 1944.

Beccaria, C. *On crimes and punishment.* Translated by Henry Paolucci. New York: Bobbs-Merrill, 1963.

Blumer, H. *Symbolic interactionism.* Englewood Cliffs, New Jersey: Prentice-Hall, Inc., 1969.

Bottomore, T. B. Marxist sociology. *International Encyclopedia of Social Sciences,* 1968, *10,* 46-53.

Brandstatter, A. F. History of police education in U. S. In W. J. Mathias (ed.), *Report of the Standards Committee.* New York: Academy of Criminal Justice Sciences, 1973.

Brantingham, P. J. Classical and positivist theory in the American criminal justice system. Unpublished mimeographed paper, Florida State University, 1971.

Briar, S., & Piliavian, I. Delinquency, situational inducements, and commitment to conformity. *Social Problems,* 1965, *13,* 35-45.

Caldwell, C. *Elements of phrenology.* New York: 1824.

Chambliss, W. J. Functional and conflict theories of crime. *MSS Modular Publications,* 1973, *17,* 1-21.

Chambliss, W. J. Toward a political economy of crime. *Theory and Society,* 1975, *2,* 152-153.

Chambliss, W. J. The state and criminal law. In William Chambliss (ed.), *Whose law? What order?* New York: Wiley and Sons, 1976, 66-106.

Chambliss, W. J. Functional and conflict theories of crime. In William Chambliss (ed.) *Whose law? What order?* New York: Wiley and Sons, 1976, 1-30.

Chambliss, W. J., & Seidman, R. *Law, order and power.* Reading: Addison-Wesley, 1971.

Cohen, A. K. *Delinquent boys: The culture of the gang.* New York: Free Press, 1955.

Cohen, A. K. The study of social disorganization and deviant behavior. In R. K. Merton et al. (eds.), *Sociologist today.* New York: Basic Books, 1959.

Cohen, A. K., & Short, J. F. Crime and juvenile delinquency. In R. K. Merton & R. Nesbet (eds.), *Contemporary social problems.* New York: Harcourt Brace Jovanovich, 1971.

Cressey, D. R. Criminological theory, social science, and the repression of crime. *Criminology,* 1978, *16*(2), 171-191.

Dahrendorf, R. Out of utopia: Toward a new orientation of sociological analysis. *American Journal of Sociology,* 1958, *64,* 115-127. (a)

Dahrendorf, R. Toward a theory of social conflict. *Journal of Conflict Resolution,* 1958, *2,* 170-183. (b)

Dahrendorf, R. *Class and class conflict in industrial society.* Stanford: Stanford University, 1959.

Davis, N. J. *Sociological constructions of deviance.* Dubuque: W. C. Brown, 1975.

della Porte, J. B. *The human physiognomy.* 1586.

de Quiros, C. B. *Modern theories of criminology.* New York: McMillan, 1967.

Denisoff, R. S., Callahan, O., Levine, M. *Theories and paradigms in contemporary sociology.* Itasca, Ill.: Peacock, 1974.

Durkheim, E. *Suicide.* New York: Free Press, 1951.

Durkheim, E. *Moral education.* New York: Free Press, 1961.

Durkheim, E. *The division of labor in society.* New York: Free Press, 1964. (a)

Durkheim, E. *The rules of the sociological method.* New York: Free Press, 1964. (b)

Durkheim, E. *The elementary forms of the religious life.* New York: Free Press, 1965.

Ferri, E. *L'omicidio-suicidio.* Rome: 1884.

Ferri, E. *The positive school of criminology.* Chicago: Charles Kerr, 1913.

Ferri, E. *Criminal society.* New York: Hafner, 1967.

Fink, A. E. *The causes of crime: Biological theories in the United States, 1800–1915.* Philadelphia: University of Pennsylvania, 1938.

Fox, V. *Introduction to criminology.* Englewood Cliffs: Prentice-Hall, 1976.

Freud, S. *A general introduction to psycho analysis.* New York: Boni, Liveright, 1920.

Freud, S. *The ego and id.* London: Hogarth, 1927.

Friedrichs, R. *A sociology of sociology.* New York: Free Press, 1970.

Gall, F. J. *Sur les fonctions du cerveau.* Paris: 1825.

Geis, G., and Meier, R. F. Looking backward and forward: Criminologists on criminology as a career. *Criminology,* 1978, *16*(2), 273–288.

Gibbons, D. C. *Society, crime and criminal careers.* Englewood Cliffs: Prentice-Hall, 1968.

Gibbons, D. C., & Garabedian, P. Conservative, liberal and radical criminology: Some trends and observations. In C. Reasons (ed.), *The criminologist: Crime and the criminal.* Pacific Palisades: Goodyear Publishing, 1974, 51–65.

Gibbons, D. C. *Society, crime and criminal careers* (3rd ed.). Englewood Cliffs: Prentice-Hall, 1977.

Gibbons, D. C. Book in preparation. 1978. (a)

Gibbons, D. C. Radical criminology revisited: Social interest, social change, and the criminal justice system. Paper presented at Pacific Sociological Association meeting, April, 1978. (b)

Glueck, S., & Glueck, E. *Unraveling juvenile delinquency.* New York: Commonwealth Fund, 1950.

Goring, C. *The English convict.* London: His Majesty's Stationery, 1913.

Gouldner, A. W. *The coming crisis of western sociology.* New York: Avon Books, 1970.

Greenberg, D. F. On one-dimensional criminology. *Theory and Society,* 1976, *3,* 610–621.

Hackler, J. The new criminology: Ideology or explanation. *Canadian Journal of Criminology and Corrections,* 1977, *19*(2), 192–195.

Hall, J. Pralegomena to the science of criminal law. *University of Pennsylvania Law Review,* 1941, 573–579.

Hall, J. Criminality. In G. Gervitch & W. V. Moore (eds.), *Twentieth century sociology.* New York: Philosophical Press, 1945.

Havelock, E. *The criminal* (2nd ed.). New York: Scribner, 1900.

Hawkins, R., & Tiedman, G. *The creation of deviance.* Columbus: Merrill, 1975.

Healy, W. *The individual delinquent.* Boston: Little, Brown, 1915.

Hobbes, T. *Leviathan.* New York: McMillan, 1947.

Hodges, D. C. Marxism as social science. Chapter 7 in M. R. Curtis (ed.), *Marxism.* New York: Atherton Press, 1970.

Hooton, E. A. *Crime and the man.* Cambridge: Harvard University Press, 1931.

Horowitz, I. L. *The rise and fall of project camelot: Studies in the relationship between social science and practical politics.* Cambridge: MIT, 1967.

Jeffery, C. R. The structure of American criminology. *Journal of Criminal Law and Criminology,* 1956, *46,* 658–672.

Jeffery, C. R. Pioneers in criminology: The historical development of criminology. *Journal of Criminal Law, Criminology and Police Science,* 1959/1960, *50,* 3–46.

Johnson, E. H. A basic error: Dealing with inmates as though they were normal. *Federal Probation,* 1971, *34,* 39–44.

Johnson, E. H. Radical criminology and Marxism: A fallible relationship. Paper presented at the Western Society of Criminology Conference, 1977, Las Vegas, Nevada.

Johnson, E. H. Praxis and radical criminology in the United States. Submitted to *Criminology* for publication, November, 1978.

Keller, R. A sociological analysis of the conflict and critical criminologies. Doctoral dissertation, University of Montana, 1976.

Klineberg, O. Mental tests. *Encyclopedia of the Social Sciences.* New York: 1933.

Kretschmer, E. *Physique and character.* New York: Cooper Square, 1925.

Krisberg, B. *Crime and privilege: Toward a new criminology.* Englewood Cliffs: Prentice-Hall, 1975.

Kuhn, T. S. *The structure of scientific revolutions* (2nd ed.). Chicago: University of Chicago, 1970.

Lemert, E. M. *Social pathology.* New York: McGraw-Hill, 1951.

Lombroso, C. *L'uomo delinquente.* Milan: 1876.

Mannheim, H. *Comparative criminology.* Boston: Houghton-Mifflin, 1965.

Maquet, J. J. *The sociology of knowledge: Its structure and its relation to the philosophy of knowledge: A critical analysis of the systems of Carl Mannheim and Pitirim Sorokin.* Boston: Beacon, 1951.

Marx, K. *Selected writings and social philosophies.* (T. B. Bottomore, trans.). London: McGraw-Hill, 1964.

Marx, K. Preface to a contribution to the critique of political economy. In K. Marx & F. Engles (eds.), *Selected works.* New York: International Publishers, 1968.

Marx, K., & Engles, F. *The German ideology.* New York: International Publishers, 1947.

Marx, K., & Engles, F. *Selected Works.* Moscow: Foreign Language Publishing House, 1962.

Marzotto, M., Platt, T., & Snare, A. A reply to Turk. *Crime and Social Justice,* 1975, *4,* 43-45.

Mason, E. J., & Bramble, W. J. *Understanding and conducting research.* New York: McGraw-Hill, 1978.

Meier, R. F. The new criminology: Continuity in criminological theory. *The Journal of Criminal Law and Criminology,* 1976, *67*(4), 461-469.

Meier, R. F. *Theories in criminology.* Beverly Hills: Sage Publications, 1977.

Merton, R. K. Social structure and anomie. *American Sociological Review,* 1938, *3,* 672-682.

Merton, R. K. *Social theory and social structure.* New York: Free Press, 1957.

Merton, R. K. *Social theory and social structure* (enlarged ed.). New York: Free Press, 1968.

Merton, R. K., & Montagu, M. F. A. Crime and the anthropologist. *American Anthropologist,* 1940, 384-408.

Miller, W. Lower-class culture as a generating milieu of gang delinquency. *Journal of Social Issues,* 1958, *14,* 5-19.

Miller, W. Ideology and criminal justice policy: Some current issues. In C. E. Reasons (ed.), *The criminologist: Crime and criminal.* Pacific Palisades: Goodyear, 1974, 19-50.

M'Naghten (10 Cl and Fin. 280), 1843.

Monachesi, E. Cesare Beccaria. In H. Mannheim (ed.), *Pioneers in criminology.* Montclair, New Jersey: Patterson Smith, 1972.

Nettler, G. *Explaining crime.* New York: McGraw-Hill, 1974.

Newman, D. J. *Introduction to criminal justice* (2nd ed.). Philadelphia: Lippincott, 1978.

Nye, F. I. *Family relationships and delinquent behavior.* New York: Wiley, 1958.

Phillipson, C. *Three criminal law reformers: Beccaria, Bentham and Romilly.* New York: 1923.

Platt, T. Prospects for a radical criminology in the United States. *Crime and Social Justice,* 1974, *1,* 2–10.

Popper, K. R. *The logic of scientific discovery.* New York: McMillan, 1959.

President's Commission on Law Enforcement and the Administration of Justice. *The challenge of crime in a free society.* Washington: Government Printing Office, 1967.

Quinney, R. *The problem of crime.* New York: Dodd Mead and Co., 1970. (a)

Quinney, R. *The social reality of crime.* Boston: Little Brown, 1970. (b)

Quinney, R. *Critique of legal order.* Boston: Little Brown, 1973.

Quinney, R. Crime control in capitalist society. In C. E. Reasons (ed.), *The criminologists.* Pacific Palisades: Goodyear Publishing, 1974.

Quinney, R. *Criminology: Analysis and critique of crime in America.* Boston: Little Brown, 1975.

Quinney, R. *Class, state, and crime.* New York: David McKay, 1977. (a)

Quinney, R. Critical and conflict criminology. Plenary session, American Society of Criminology, November, 1977. (b)

Radcliff-Brown, A. R. *Structure and functions in primitive society.* Glencoe: Free Press, 1956.

Radzinowicz, L. *In search of criminology.* Cambridge: Harvard University, 1962.

Ray, I. *A treatise on the medical jurisprudence of insanity* (3rd ed.). Boston: 1885.

Reasons, C. E. *The criminologist: Crime and criminal.* Pacific Palisades: Goodyear, 1974.

Reasons, C. E. Social thought and social structure: The criminologist, crime and the criminal. In C. E. Reasons (ed.), *The criminologist: crime and the criminal.* Pacific Palisades: Goodyear, 1974, 1–18.

Reasons, C. E. Social thought and social structures. *Criminology,* 1975, *13,* 332–365.

Reasons, C. E., and Rich, R. M. *The sociology of law: A conflict perspective.* Toronto: Butterworth, 1978.

Reckless, W. A new theory of delinquency and crime. *Federal Probation,* 1961, *25,* 42–46.

Reckless, W. *The crime problem* (5th ed.). New York: Appleton, Century Crofts, 1973.

Reid, S. T. *Crime and criminology.* Hinsdale: Dryden, 1976.

Reiss, A. J. Delinquency and the failure of personal and social controls. *American Sociological Review,* 1951, *16,* 196–207.

Reiss, A. J. Social correlates of psychological types of delinquency. *American Sociological Review,* 1952, *17,* 710–718.

Reynolds, L. T., & Reynolds, J. M. (eds.). *The sociology of sociology.* New York: David McKay, 1969.

Schafer, S. *Theories in criminology.* New York: Random House, 1969.

Schafer, S. *Introduction to criminology.* Reston: Reston Publishing Co., 1976.

Schrag, C. *Crime and justice American style.* Washington: Government Printing Office, 1971.

Schur, E. M. *Labeling deviant behavior.* New York: Harper and Row, 1971.

Schwendinger, H. Editorial. *Crime and Social Justice,* 1974, *1,* 1.

Schwendinger, H., and Schwendinger, J. Defenders of order or guardians of human rights? In Taylor et al. (eds.), *Critical criminology.* London: Routeledge and Kegan Paul, 1975.

Schwendinger, H., and Schwendinger, J. Social class and the definition of crime. *Crime and Social Justice,* 1977, *4,* 4–13.

Sellin, T. The Lombrosian myth in criminology. *American Journal of Sociology,* 1937, *42,* 896–897.

Sellin, T. Culture, conflict and crime. *Social Science Research Council Bulletin,* 1938, *41,* 1–7.

Shaw, C. R., & McKay, H. D. (eds.) *Juvenile delinquency and urban areas* (revised ed.) Chicago: University of Chicago, 1969.

Sheldon, W. H. *Varieties of delinquent youth.* New York: Harper, 1949.

Spector, M., & Kitsusu, J. I. *Constructing social problems.* Menlo Park: Cummings, 1977.

Stinchcombe, A. L. *Rebellion in a high school.* Chicago: Quadrangle, 1964.

Sutherland, E. H. *Criminology.* Philadelphia: Lippincott, 1924.

Sutherland, E. H. *White collar crime.* New York: Holt, Rinehard & Winston, 1949.

Sutherland, E. H., & Cressey, D. *Principles of criminology* (7th ed.). Philadelphia: Lippincott, 1970.

Sutherland, E. H., & Cressey, D. *Criminology* (10th ed.). Philadelphia: Lippincott, 1978.

Sykes, G. The rise of critical criminology. *Journal of Criminal Law and Criminology,* 1971, *65,* 206–213.

Sykes, G., & Matza, D. Techniques of neutralization: A the-

Swank, C. J. A descriptive analysis of criminal justice doctoral program in the United States. Doctoral dissertation, Michigan State University, 1972.

ory of delinquency. *American Sociological Review,* 1957, *22,* 664-670.

Takagi, P. Personal interview. New Orleans, Louisiana, March, 1978.

Tannenbaum, F. *Crime and the community.* Boston: Ginn, 1938.

Tappan, P. W. Who is the criminal? *American Sociological Review,* 1947, *12,* 101-109.

Taylor, I. and Young, J. Personal interview. Hamilton, Ontario: McMaster University, May, 1978.

Taylor, I., Walton, P., & Young, J. *The new criminology.* London: Routledge and Kegan Paul, 1973.

Taylor, I., Walton, P., & Young, J. *Critical criminology.* London: Routledge and Kegan Paul, 1975. (a)

Taylor, I., Walton, P., & Young, J. Critical criminology in Britain: Review and prospects. In Taylor et al. (eds.), *Critical criminology.* London: Routledge and Kegan Paul, 1975. (b)

Thomas, W. I. *The child in America.* New York: Knopf, 1928.

Thrasher, F. *The gang.* Chicago: University of Chicago, 1927.

Turk, A. T. Conflict and criminality. *American Sociological Review,* 1966, *31,* 34-39.

Turk, A. T. *Criminality and legal order.* Chicago: Rand McNally, 1969.

Turk, A. T. Prospects and pitfalls for radical criminology: A critical response to Platt. *Crime and Social Justice,* 1975, *4,* 41-42.

Turk, A. T. Law as a weapon in social conflict. *Social Problems,* 1976, *23,* 276-291.

Turk, A. T. Class conflict in criminalization. *Sociological Focus,* 1977, *10,* 209-220.

Turk, A. T. Analyzing official deviance. Unpublished paper, 1978.

Vold, G. B. *Theoretical criminology.* New York: Oxford University, 1958.

Warren, R. L. The sociology of knowledge in the problems of the inner city. *Social Science Quarterly,* 1971, *52,* 465-475.

Wellford, C. S. Labeling theory in criminology: An assessment. *Social Problems,* 1975, *22,* 332-345.

Whyte, W. F. *Street corner society.* Chicago: University of Chicago, 1943.

Wolfgang, M. Pioneers in criminology: Cesare Lombroso (1835-1909). *Journal of Criminal Law, Criminology and Police Science,* 1961, *52,* 361-369.

Wolfgang, M. Criminology and the criminologists. *Journal of Criminal Law, Criminology and Police Science,* 1963, *54,* 155-162.

Wolfgang, M. Developments in criminology in the United States with some comments on the future. Paper presented at the Fifth National Conference, Institute of Criminology, University of Cambridge, England, July, 1973.

Zeitun, I. M. *Ideology and the development of sociological theory.* Englewood Cliffs: Prentice-Hall, 1968.

Zinn, H. *The politics of history.* Boston: Beard, 1970.

Index

Anomie
    conformity and, 37-38
    deviancy and, 37-38
    opportunity theory and, 39-40
Beccaria, Cesare
    criminal justice reformer as, 2-3
    criminology, classical school of and, 2-4
    Essay on Crimes and Punishment, 1-2
    "greatest good to greatest number," 3
    social contract theory, 2-3
Bentham, Jeremy
    criminology, classical school of, 3-4
    felicific calculus of, 3-4
    "greatest good to greatest number," 3
Binet, Alfred
    Binet-Simon intelligence test, 29
    Stanford-Binet intelligence test, 29
Chambliss, William
    conflict criminology, 70-73
Commandments, biblical
    pity, 2
    probity, 2
Conflict criminology, 60-73
    appellate courts and, 69-70
    Chambliss, William on, 70-73
    criminal justice system and, 70-71
    legal order and, 69
Conflict functionalism
    Dahrendorf, Ralf as proponent of, 59-60

Conflict perspective, 17-20
  criminality and, 19-20
Courts
  appellate, 69-70
Crime
  control of, and critical criminology, 77
  critical criminology and, 77-81
  definitions of, 79-81
  function of, 16
  functionalism and, 16-17
  legal definition of, 90
  occupational, 94-95
  social reality of, 79-81
  white collar, 94-95
Criminal justice
  criminology vs., 52-53
  discipline, as a, 51-52
  law, emphasis upon, 53
Criminal justice system, 81-83
  bias within, 70-71
Criminal law, 13-14
  impartiality of, 3
Criminality
  biological theories of, 21-27
  conflict theory and, 19-20
  label theory view of, 66
  psychological theories of, 25, 27-31
  sociological theories of, 31-49
Criminals
  atavistic, 7
  biological inferiority theories, 21-27
  classification of, 6-7
  psychological inferiority theories, 25, 27-31

Criminology
　biological theories of, 21-27
　classical school of, 2-5
　　famous persons influencing, 4
　　tenets of, 4-5
　　positive school, vs., 10-11
　Conflict. *See* Conflict Criminology
　crime, legal definition of and, 90
　Critical. *See* Critical Criminology
　differential association theory, 44-46
　　weaknesses of, 46
　emergence of, 1
　Freud, Sigmund, 29-30
　functional perspective. *See* Functionalism
　future of, 95-98
　"Holy Three" of positive school, 6-10
　human rights and, 1
　labeling theory, 46-49
　　symbolic interactionism and, 47
　　tenets of, 47-48
　law, emphasis upon, 53
　New. *See* New Criminology
　objectives of, 1
　phrenology and, 22-23
　positive school of, 5-11, 21
　　contributors to, 6
　　effects of science on, 5-6
　psychological theories of, 25, 27-31
　　positivistic school and, 27
　Radical. *See* Radical Criminology
　sociological theories of, 31-49
　　control, 32-36
　　cultural deviance, 41-43
　　strain, 36-41
　　symbolic interactionism, 43-49

Criminology—*(Continued)*
    sociology of, 13-14
    tenets of, 51-52
    witchcraft, punishment for practice of, 28
        classical school and, 28
Critical Criminology, 73-87
    capitalism and, 77-78
    class conflict and, 75-77
    crime and, 77-81
    crime control and, 77
    crime, definitions of, 79-81
    criminal justice and, 81-83
    criminal law theory and, 75-77
    "critique" and, 86-87
    deviance, social theory of, 84-85
    new criminology and, 74, 83, 86
    perspective, as a, 73
    Quinney, Richard on, 74-82
    social reality of crime, 79-81
    "system" and, 73
Darwin, Charles
    biological determinism, 5-6
Delinquency
    concentric circle theory of, 42
    control theory of, 35-36
    gangs, inner-city, 42
    non-biological causes of, 28, 30-49
    subculture of, 39-42
Deviance
    anomie and, 37-38
    cultural theory of, 41-43
        symbolic interactionism, vs. 45-46
    cultural conflict theory of, 43
    modes of adaptation to, 37-41
    social theory of, by Dahrendorf, Quinney, Turk, Vold, 85
    theory of, by Turk, Austin, 67-68

Engels, Frederick
  conflict theory of, 17-20
Ferri, Enrico
  criminal classification by, 8
  criminology, positive school of and, 8-9
  Ferri Draft of 1921, 8-9
  "Holy Three" of positivistic criminology and, 6, 8-9
  publications of, 8
Freud, Sigmund, 29-30
Functionalism
  concepts of, 15-17
  correctional treatment, effect upon, 17
  crime and, 16-17
  value consensus and, 17
Gall, Franz Joseph
  phrenology, creator of, 22-23
Garofalo, Raffaele
  crime, defined by, 9
  criminal theory of, 9
  criminological biological studies of, 24-25
  criminology, positive school of, and, 9-10
  "Holy Three" of positivistic criminology and, 6
  psychic anomaly, 9
Hedonism
  principle of, 3
Hobbes, Thomas, 1
Hooton, Ernest A.
  criminological biological studies of, 25
Human rights
  social order and, 1
Ink Blot Test, 31
Lawlessness. *See* Anomie
Law enforcement
  discriminatory, 94

Lombrosco, Cesare
    atavistic criminal, 7
    criminal classification by, 6-8
    criminology, positive school of and, 6-8
    degeneracy theory of by, 23-24
    "Holy Three" of positivistic criminology and, 6-8

Marx, Karl
    capitalistic society of, 57-58
    class conflict, 56-58
    conflict theory of, 17-20
    economic organization, effects of on society, 55-58
    man, alienation of, 56
    social conflict, 55-60

Natural morality, 10

New Criminology, 51, 53-60, 86
    conflict theory as basis for, 54-60
    critical criminology and, 83
    criticisms of, 91-93, 97-98
    myths of, 94-95

Order, legal, 69

Phrenology, 22-23

Physiognomy, 22

Praxis, 87, 89-90, 96

Quinney, Richard
    capitalism, dialectic within, 77-78
    crime, social reality theory of by, 79-81
    crime control, 77-78
    criminal justice system, 81-83
        weaknesses of, 82
    criminal law, theory of, 75-76
    critical criminology, 73-87, 83
        theories of, 75
    Marxist attitudes of, 74
    publications of, 74

Radical Criminology, 13, 87-91
    academia and, 87
    characteristics of, 88-89
    Marxist basis for, 87
    political commitment within, 89, 91
    praxis, 89-90
Simon, Theodore
    Binet-Simon intelligence test, 29
Social contract, 2-3
Sociology
    Chicago School of, 41
    conflict theory. *See* Conflict theory; Marx, Karl; Engels, Frederick
    dialectical conflict perspective, 59
    functional perspective. *See* Functionalism
    Marx, Karl, contributions to, 54-58
    revolution within, 12
Society
    conflict model of, 69
Spencer, Herbert, 15
Stanford-Binet intelligence test, 29
Suicide, *anomique,* 37
Turk, Austin
    class conflict, 66
    conflict criminology and, 64-68
    criminality, 66
    deviance theory of, 67-68
    labeling theory, 65-67
        opinion of, 66
Vold, George
    conflict criminology and, 60-64
    naturalistic theories of, 62-63
    social conflict, 60-62
    society, concept of, 61
Witchcraft
    punishment for practice of, 28